YOUR LIFE, YOUR CHOICE

DR AKHILESH DWIVEDI

Made with ❤ on the Notion Press Platform
www.notionpress.com

Dedicated to

"My Loving Parents and Lord Sita-Ram Hanuman "

Contents

Contents

Preface

In today's fast-paced world, it can be easy to feel overwhelmed and lost, as though you're simply going through the motions and not making much progress. But what if you could take control of your life and shape your own future? What if you could be your own boss and work on what you're passionate about?

In this book, we explore the powerful concept of "Your life, Your Choice" and how it can be applied to the idea of "be your own boss". By taking responsibility for your own life and making informed decisions, you can create a fulfilling and meaningful future for yourself. Through inspiring stories and practical advice, we will show you how to identify your passions and goals, develop a plan to achieve them, and take action to turn your dreams into reality. We will also explore the challenges and obstacles you may face along the way and provide strategies for overcoming them.

Whether you're just starting out on your entrepreneurial journey or looking to make a change in your life, this book will provide the tools and inspiration you need to take control of your life and be your own boss. So, get ready to take the first step towards a brighter future and make the choices that will help you lead the life you want. People should read the book "Your Life Your Choice" because it offers valuable insights and practical advice on how to take control of their lives and make informed decisions that lead to a fulfilling and meaningful future. The book is designed for anyone who wants to:

Discover their passions and goals: By reading this book, people can learn how to identify what they're truly passionate about and what their goals are, and how to turn these passions and goals into a plan of action. Be their own boss: The book provides inspiration and guidance on how to start a business or take control of their careers, and how to make the choices that are right for them. It shows that anyone can be their own boss and work on what they love, with the right mind-set and strategies.

Overcome challenges: The book acknowledges that starting a business or taking control of your life can be challenging, but provides practical strategies for overcoming obstacles and building resilience.

Live a fulfilling life: By following the advice in this book, people can learn how to lead a life that is fulfilling, meaningful, and true to their values. They can take control of their future and create the life they want, rather than simply going through the motions.

In conclusion, the book "Your Life Your Choice" is a valuable resource for anyone looking to take control of their life and shape their own future. Whether you're just starting out on your entrepreneurial journey or looking to make a change in your life, this book provides the tools and inspiration you need to be your own boss and lead the life you want.

CHAPTER ONE

Learning Success

"Any fool can know. The point is to understand." — Albert Einstein

As everyone has its own personal experiences or choices, however, lets redefine and understand the concept of "life" and "choice" in context of success.

In general, the phrase "Your life, your choice" means that individuals have the right to make their own decisions and choices in life, and that they are responsible for the consequences of those choices. It emphasizes the idea of personal freedom and agency, and encourages people to take control of their own lives and shape their own future.

However, it's important to keep in mind that choices and actions can have both positive and negative impacts, not just on oneself, but also on others and the environment. So, making informed and responsible choices can lead to a more fulfilling and meaningful life.

Once upon a time, there was a young woman named Natalia who worked as an employee at a large corporation. Although she was good at her job and received a steady pay check, she felt unfulfilled and trapped. She longed to be her own boss, to have the freedom and autonomy to make her own decisions and shape her future.

One day, Natalia came across the phrase "be your own boss" and it struck a chord with her. She realized that she had the power to take control of her life and make her own rules, instead of being beholden to someone else. She decided to take the leap and start her own business.

Natalia was not sure where to begin, but she was determined to make it work. She spent countless hours researching her market, gathering information on her competition, and developing a business plan. She also sought out advice from other entrepreneurs and business experts, to help her make the best decisions.

With hard work and persistence, Natalia's business took off. She was now in charge of her own success and had the freedom to make the choices that were best for her and her business. She was able to work on projects that she was passionate about, and she was finally doing what she loved.

And as her business grew, so did Natalia's confidence and sense of purpose. She felt proud of what she had accomplished and was grateful for the opportunity to be her own boss. She also inspired others to follow in her footsteps, to take control of their lives and pursue their own passions.

From that day on, Natalia lived her life with the motto "be your own boss" in mind, always striving to make the best decisions for herself and her business, and to live the life she had always dreamed of.

Once upon a time, there was a young man named Bruce who was not sure what he wanted to do with his life. He felt like he was just going through the motions and not making much progress. One day, he heard someone say the phrase "Your life, your choice," and it really resonated with him.

He realized that he had been passively allowing life to happen to him, instead of actively shaping his own future. He decided to take control of his life and make some choices that would lead him towards his goals and aspirations.

First, Bruce identified what he was passionate about and what he wanted to achieve. He wrote down his long-term goals and broke them down into smaller, achievable steps. He also made a plan for how he was going to reach those goals, taking into account his strengths, weaknesses, and available resources.

Next, Bruce took action. He started taking small, incremental steps towards his goals every day, learning new skills and seeking out opportunities that would help him get closer to where he wanted to be. He surrounded himself with supportive people who encouraged and inspired him, and he remained focused and committed to his goals, no matter what obstacles he faced.

With time, Bruce's hard work and determination paid off. He achieved one goal after another, and he finally found the success and fulfilment he had been searching for. He was proud of himself for taking control of his life and making choices that had led him to where he was.

And so, Bruce lived the rest of his life with the motto "Your life, your choice" in mind, always making decisions that would bring him closer to his goals and help him lead the life he wanted. And he inspired others to do the same, helping them take control of their lives and achieve their own dreams.

Natalia and Bruce could be your role model for success in life or anyone else who is nearby you who is inspiring you most.

Learning from successful people can be a valuable way to gain insights into what it takes to achieve your own goals. By studying the habits, attitudes, and approaches of successful individuals, you can gain a better understanding of what has worked for them and what you can do to increase your chances of success. Here are a few tips for learning from successful people:

Seek out role models: Identify individuals who embody the qualities and characteristics you admire and would like to emulate. These could be people in your personal life, or they could be public figures.

Read about their lives: Read biographies, autobiographies, and other accounts of the lives of successful people to gain a deeper understanding of what they have achieved and how they have done it.

Watch interviews and speeches: Many successful people have given interviews and speeches in which they discuss their experiences, challenges, and philosophies. These can be a great way to learn from their insights and perspectives.

Ask questions: If you have the opportunity to meet or interact with successful individuals, don't be afraid to ask them questions about their experiences and what they have learned.

Emulate what works: Pay attention to the habits and behaviors that successful people seem to have in common, and consider incorporating these into your own life.

It's important to remember that success is a highly personal and subjective concept, and what works for one person may not work for another. However, by learning from successful individuals and adapting their insights to your own life and goals, you can increase your chances of success.

CHAPTER TWO

Success is Predictable

"The more I read, the more I acquire, the more certain I am that I know nothing." — Voltaire

Once upon a time, there was a young man named Steve who lived in a small village. Steve was very ambitious and always strived to be successful. He had heard from many people that success was predictable, and he firmly believed in this idea. He would spend hours reading books and talking to successful people, trying to figure out the secrets to their success.

However, despite his best efforts, Steve was not able to achieve the success that he desired. He felt like he was always one step behind, no matter how hard he tried. He was frustrated and disappointed, and he started to lose hope.

One day, Steve decided to take a break from his pursuit of success and went on a journey to rediscover himself. He traveled to different parts of the world, met new people, and learned about different cultures and lifestyles.

During his journey, Steve realized that success was not predictable after all. He realized that success was a journey, not a destination. He also discovered that the most important aspect of success was not what he achieved but how he lived his life. He realized that the true meaning of success was to live life to the fullest, to be happy, and to make a positive impact on the world.

When Steve returned to his village, he was a changed man. He was no longer obsessed with success and instead, he focused on finding happiness and fulfillment in his everyday life. He also made an effort to help others in his village, and his actions inspired many people to follow his lead.

In the end, Steve realized that success was not about achieving a certain goal, but about finding happiness and fulfillment in life. He discovered that the secret to success was to rediscover oneself and to live life to the fullest. And so, Steve lived the rest of his life with joy and contentment, inspiring others to do the same.

The moral of the story is that success is not predictable, but it can be found by rediscovering oneself and finding happiness and fulfillment in life. So, don't be afraid to take a break from your pursuit of success and go on a journey to rediscover yourself. The truth of success will reveal itself in due time.

Success is not completely predictable, as there are many factors that can influence an individual's path to success, including luck, timing, and opportunities. However, there are certain traits and habits that successful individuals tend to have in common, and these can increase the likelihood of success.

For example, successful people tend to have a clear vision of what they want to achieve, a strong work ethic, a positive attitude, and a willingness to take calculated risks. They also often have a strong support system, a growth mind-set, and the ability to learn from failures and setbacks.

While these traits and habits can increase the likelihood of success, they do not guarantee it. There are many individuals who possess these qualities but still struggle to achieve their goals, and there are others who achieve great success without exhibiting all of these traits.

So, while success is not entirely predictable, it is possible to increase your chances of success by developing the traits and habits that are commonly associated with successful individuals.

Rediscovering oneself is a common theme in personal development and can be a valuable journey for many people. The process of rediscovery involves taking a step back, reflecting on one's values, beliefs, and goals, and reassessing the direction one is heading in life. It can help individuals gain a better understanding of who they are and what they truly want out of life.

By rediscovering oneself, individuals can gain a greater sense of purpose, clarify their values and priorities, and make decisions that align with their true self. It can also help to alleviate feelings of dissatisfaction, confusion, or boredom and lead to increased happiness and fulfilment.

That being said, rediscovery is not the only truth, and it may not be the right path for everyone. For some, simply living in the present moment and focusing on what brings them joy and satisfaction may be enough.

Ultimately, the most important thing is to find what works for you and what helps you lead a fulfilling and meaningful life. Whether that involves rediscovery or not, the truth is subjective and will be different for each individual.

CHAPTER THREE

Be Selective!!

"Don't just teach your children to read. Teach them to question what they read. Teach them to question everything." — George Carlin

Once upon a time, there was a young woman named Sarah who had always dreamed of starting her own business. She had a passion for fashion and wanted to use her creativity to design unique clothing that would make people feel confident and beautiful.

One day, Sarah finally decided to take the leap and start her own business. She was determined to be her own boss and make her dream a reality. However, she soon realized that starting a business was not as easy as she thought. There were countless decisions to make and a lot of work to be done.

At first, Sarah was eager to take on every opportunity that came her way. She said yes to every project, no matter how big or small, and worked tirelessly to get everything done. However, as time went by, she started to feel overwhelmed and stressed. She was working long hours, and her quality of life was suffering.

It was then that Sarah realized that she needed to be selective about the opportunities she took on. She realized that in order to be a successful business owner, she needed to prioritize her time and energy, and only take on projects that aligned with her goals and values.

Sarah started to be more mindful about the opportunities she said yes to, and she was amazed at the difference it made. She was able to focus on the projects that were important to her, and her business began to grow. She was also able to take better care of herself and maintain a healthy work-life balance.

In the end, Sarah's business was a huge success. People loved her unique clothing, and she was proud of what she had accomplished. She realized that being her own boss was not just about making decisions and taking on opportunities; it was also about being selective and making choices that aligned with her goals and values.

The moral of the story is that to be a successful business owner, one needs to be selective about the opportunities they take on. It's important to prioritize time and energy and only take on projects that align with your goals and values. Being your own boss is not just about making decisions, but about making the right decisions.

Being your own boss can be a rewarding and fulfilling experience, but it also requires a great deal of responsibility and effort. To be successful as an entrepreneur or small business owner, it is important to be selective and make informed decisions. Here are a few things to consider:

Choose the right business idea: Identify a business idea that aligns with your skills, interests, and values, and that has a viable market. Conduct thorough research and feasibility analysis before starting your business.

Develop a solid business plan: A well-written business plan can help you stay focused and organized, and can also be used to secure funding and attract investors.

Be strategic with finances: Be mindful of your finances, including expenses, revenue, and cash flow. Make smart investments, seek out funding opportunities, and be prepared for financial setbacks.

Build a strong team: Surround yourself with people who have the skills, experience, and passion to help your business succeed. Consider hiring employees, forming partnerships, or seeking out advisors.

Stay focused and disciplined: Running a business requires hard work, dedication, and perseverance. Stay focused on your goals and be disciplined in your approach to work and decision-making.

By being selective and strategic in these areas, you can increase your chances of success as a small business owner or entrepreneur. However, it's important to remember that starting a business is a risk, and there are no guarantees of success. Nevertheless, for those who are willing to put in the effort, being your own boss can be a fulfilling and rewarding experience.

One need to take action immediately

Taking action is an important aspect of being your own boss. Taking prompt and decisive action can help you overcome obstacles, seize opportunities, and make progress towards your goals.

However, it's also important to balance taking action with careful planning and strategic thinking. Taking action without proper preparation can lead to mistakes and setbacks, so it's important to take the time to do your research, create a solid business plan, and make informed decisions.

Here are a few tips for taking action as a small business owner or entrepreneur:

Set clear goals and priorities: Identify what you want to achieve and develop a plan for how to get there.

Be proactive: Take the initiative to seek out opportunities, solve problems, and make things happen.

Take calculated risks: Be willing to take risks, but also be mindful of the potential consequences. Consider seeking advice from experienced business owners or financial advisors.

Stay flexible: Be open to change and be prepared to pivot your strategy if needed.

Celebrate progress and successes: Celebrate your wins and acknowledge your progress, no matter how small. This will help keep you motivated and focused.

By taking action, being proactive, and staying focused on your goals, you can increase your chances of success as a small business owner or entrepreneur. But remember, success takes time, and there will be challenges and setbacks along the way. The key is to remain focused, stay disciplined, and keep taking action towards your goals.

CHAPTER FOUR

Habits of Success

"A man who reads too much and uses his own brain too little falls into lazy habits of thinking." — Albert Einstein

Once upon a time, there was a young man named Wade who was always fascinated by the idea of being his own boss. He dreamed of starting his own business, setting his own hours, and being in control of his financial future. However, Wade didn't know how to make his dream a reality. He was good at his day job, but he wasn't sure he had what it takes to be a successful entrepreneur.

One day, Wade stumbled upon a book that changed his life. The book was about developing the habits of successful people, and Wade was amazed by the insights he gained from reading it. He learned that success was not just about having a good idea or knowing how to do something well, but it was also about having the right habits and mindset.

Wade started to apply the principles he learned from the book to his daily life. He became more organized, set goals for himself, and prioritized his time more effectively. He also made a habit of seeking out new opportunities and challenging himself to try new things.

As Wade's habits started to change, he noticed that his confidence was growing. He felt more in control of his life and was making progress towards his goal of starting his own business. He started networking with other entrepreneurs and researching different business opportunities.

One day, Wade found a business opportunity that he was passionate about and decided to take the leap and start his own company. It wasn't easy, but with the habits he had developed, he was able to overcome the challenges and build a successful business.

Years later, Wade was running a thriving company, and he was proud of what he had accomplished. He looked back on his journey and was grateful for the lessons he learned and the habits he developed along the way. He was now his own boss, and he lived a life of financial freedom and fulfillment.

In conclusion, Wade's story teaches us that to be your own boss, one needs to develop the habits of success. Habits like setting goals, being organized, seeking out new opportunities, and having a growth mindset are essential for entrepreneurs to succeed. With hard work and determination, anyone can turn their dream of being their own boss into a reality.

Developing successful habits is crucial for anyone who wants to be their own boss. Habits are the building blocks of success, and they can help you achieve your goals and reach your full potential. Here are a few habits that can help you as a small business owner or entrepreneur:

Be proactive: Take the initiative to seek out opportunities, solve problems, and make things happen.

Set clear goals and prioritize: Identify what you want to achieve and develop a plan for how to get there.

Stay organized and focused: Keep track of your tasks, set deadlines, and prioritize your work. Stay focused on what's important and avoid distractions.

Build a strong network: Surround yourself with people who have the skills, experience, and passion to help your business succeed. Consider hiring employees, forming partnerships, or seeking out advisors.

Continuously learn and improve: Stay current with industry trends and advancements, seek out new opportunities for growth, and be willing to adapt to change.

Maintain a positive attitude: Keep a positive and optimistic outlook, even in the face of challenges and setbacks. Believe in yourself and your abilities.

Be disciplined and consistent: Be disciplined in your approach to work, decision-making, and following through on your commitments. Consistency is key to success.

By developing these habits, you can increase your chances of success as a small business owner or entrepreneur. But remember, success takes time and effort, and developing successful habits is an ongoing process that requires discipline and commitment.

CHAPTER FIVE

Positive Addiction

"All of the books in the world contain no more information than is broadcast as video in a single large American city in a single year. Not all bits have equal value." — Carl Sagan

Once upon a time, there was a young woman named Emily who always felt like she was stuck in a rut. She worked a 9-5 job that she didn't enjoy, and she felt like she was just going through the motions day after day. Despite her unhappiness, she was afraid to make a change because she didn't know what else to do.

One day, Emily was introduced to the concept of developing a positive addiction. The idea was to find something that you were passionate about and make it a daily habit. The more you did it, the more you would look forward to it and the happier you would become.

Emily was intrigued by the idea and decided to give it a try. She started by making a list of things she enjoyed and activities that made her feel good. Eventually, she landed on photography and decided to make it her positive addiction.

She started taking her camera with her everywhere she went and taking photos of anything and everything that caught her eye. She found joy in capturing the beauty of the world around her, and she was amazed at how much her mood improved when she was taking photos.

As Emily's passion for photography grew, she started to dream of making it her career. She took classes, read books, and practiced every day. Eventually, her work was good enough that she was able to start selling her photos and making a name for herself.

Years later, Emily was running a successful photography business and was doing something she loved every day. She was her own boss, and she never felt like she was just going through the motions. She was grateful for the positive addiction she had developed and the impact it had on her life.

In conclusion, Emily's story teaches us that to be your own boss, one needs to develop a positive addiction. By finding something you are passionate about and making it a daily habit, you can find joy in your work and create a fulfilling career. With hard work and determination, anyone can turn their passion into a successful business and be their own boss.

Developing a positive addiction can be an important factor in the success of someone who wants to be their own boss. A positive addiction refers to a habit or activity that is beneficial to your health, well-being, and success. By developing a positive addiction, you can increase your chances of success as a small business owner or entrepreneur.

Here are a few examples of positive addictions that can help you in your entrepreneurial journey:

Exercise: Regular exercise can improve your physical and mental health, increase your energy levels, and boost your mood.

Reading: Reading can expand your knowledge, stimulate your creativity, and help you stay informed about your industry and market.

Networking: Building a strong network of contacts can help you find new opportunities, connect with potential customers, and receive support and advice from other business owners.

Personal development: Investing in your personal growth through education, training, and coaching can help you develop new skills and improve your overall performance.

Meditation or mindfulness: Practicing mindfulness or meditation can help you reduce stress, increase focus, and improve your overall well-being.

By incorporating these positive addictions into your daily routine, you can improve your chances of success as a small business owner or entrepreneur. However, it's important to find a balance and avoid developing addictions that may negatively impact your health, relationships, or business. The key is to find habits that work for you and that align with your goals and values.

CHAPTER SIX

Avoid Shortcuts

"There are four powers: memory and intellect, desire and covetousness. The two first are mental and the others sensual. The three senses sight, hearing, and smell cannot well be prevented; touch and taste not at all." — Leonardo da Vinci

Once upon a time, there was a young man named Stephen who dreamed of being his own boss. He was tired of working long hours for someone else and wanted the freedom to make his own decisions and control his own life.

So, he quit his job and started his own business. He was determined to make it a success and was willing to work hard to achieve his dream. But as time went on, Stephen started to feel the pressure of running a business and the temptation to take shortcuts to save time and effort.

One day, Stephen was approached by a stranger who offered him a solution to all his problems. The stranger promised that if Stephen used his shortcuts, he would be able to save time and make more money. Stephen was tempted and considered taking the offer, but then he remembered his goal of being his own boss.

He realized that being his own boss meant taking responsibility for his own actions and not relying on anyone else to make his decisions. He also realized that taking shortcuts would not only be unethical, but it would also undermine the foundation of his business.

So, Stephen turned down the offer and continued to work hard, building his business with integrity and honesty. He made mistakes along the way, but he learned from them and continued to grow. Eventually, his hard work paid. He knew that true success could only be achieved through hard work, determination, and a strong moral compass.

Years went by, and Stephen's business continued to thrive. He had employees of his own, but he never forgot the lessons he learned on his journey to becoming his own boss. He taught his employees the importance of taking the right path and making ethical decisions, and his business became known as one of the most honest and successful companies in the industry.

In the end, Stephen was grateful for the challenges he faced and the lessons he learned. He knew that taking shortcuts would have only led to temporary success, but by following the right path, he was able to build a legacy that would last a lifetime.

And so, Stephen's story serves as a reminder that to truly be your own boss, one must take no shortcuts and always strive to make ethical decisions. True success and happiness can only be achieved through hard work, determination, and a strong moral compass.

Taking shortcuts can be tempting, especially when you're trying to get ahead or meet deadlines. However, taking shortcuts can have negative consequences in the long term and can damage your reputation, relationships, and business.

As a small business owner or entrepreneur, it's important to focus on building a strong foundation and creating long-term success, rather than taking shortcuts that may compromise your values or harm your business. Here are a few reasons why taking shortcuts can be harmful:

Compromised quality: Taking shortcuts often means cutting corners, which can result in subpar work and a decline in the quality of your products or services.

Reputation damage: When you take shortcuts, it can become evident to your customers, partners, and employees. This can harm your reputation and make it harder to build trust and credibility in the future.

Decreased motivation: Taking shortcuts can lead to a lack of motivation and a decline in the overall performance of your business. When you take the easy way out, it can become harder to find the drive and determination to continue working hard and reaching your goals.

Missed opportunities: Taking shortcuts can prevent you from discovering new opportunities and experiences. By focusing solely on the end result, you may miss out on the learning and growth that comes from taking the time to do things the right way.

Instead of taking shortcuts, focus on building a strong foundation and creating long-term success by doing things the right way. This means putting in the time, effort, and dedication needed to achieve your goals. By taking a disciplined and honest approach, you can increase your chances of success as a small business owner or entrepreneur.

One need to take decisions with discipline and determination

Making decisions with discipline and determination is an important aspect of being your own boss. As a small business owner or entrepreneur, you are in charge of your own success, and the decisions you make can have a significant impact on the future of your business.

Here are a few ways to make decisions with discipline and determination:

Define your values and priorities: Determine what is important to you and your business, and use this as a guide for making decisions. This can help you stay focused and make decisions that align with your values and goals.

Gather information: Take the time to research and gather information about the options available to you. This can help you make informed decisions that are based on facts and evidence, rather than assumptions or guesses.

Consider the consequences: Think about the potential outcomes of your decisions and the impact they may have on your business and the people around you. This can help you weigh the pros and cons and make decisions that are in the best interests of your business.

Trust your instincts: Sometimes, despite all the research and planning, the best course of action may not be clear. In these situations, trust your instincts and make a decision based on your gut feeling.

Be confident and decisive: Once you have made a decision, have the discipline and determination to see it through. Be confident in your choices and take action, rather than second-guessing yourself.

By making decisions with discipline and determination, you can increase your chances of success as a small business owner or entrepreneur. Remember, being your own boss requires taking risks and making tough choices, but by being disciplined and determined, you can navigate these challenges and achieve your goals.

CHAPTER SEVEN

Visualise Yourself as You Want to Be

"There is no end to education. It is not that you read a book, pass an examination, and finish with education. The whole of life, from the moment you are born to the moment you die, is a process of learning." — Jiddu Krishnamurti

Once upon a time, there was a young woman named Sarah who was tired of working for someone else. She had big dreams of starting her own business and being her own boss, but she didn't know where to start.

One day, Sarah came across a quote that said, "If you can see it in your mind, you can hold it in your hand." She realized that in order to become her own boss, she needed to first visualize herself as the successful business owner she wanted to be.

So, Sarah closed her eyes and began to picture herself running her own business. She imagined herself making decisions, leading her team, and watching her business grow. She saw herself as confident, capable, and in control.

With this new visualization in mind, Sarah began to take action. She made a plan, did research, and took small steps every day to bring her dream to life. Despite the challenges she faced, Sarah remained focused on her vision and never gave up.

As time passed, Sarah's vision became a reality. Her business was thriving, and she was finally her own boss. She was amazed at how much she had accomplished and was grateful for the power of visualization.

Sarah never forgot the impact that visualization had on her journey to becoming her own boss. She began to share her story with others and encourage them to use the power of visualization to reach their goals. And, just like Sarah, many of them found success and happiness by seeing themselves as they wanted to be.

In the end, Sarah's story serves as a reminder that to truly be your own boss, one must first visualize themselves as they want to be. By using the power of visualization, you can bring your dreams to life and achieve success beyond your wildest dreams.

Visualization is a powerful tool for personal and professional development, and it can be particularly useful for entrepreneurs and small business owners. By visualizing yourself as you want to be, you can create a clear picture of your future and use it to motivate and inspire you to take action.

Here are a few ways to use visualization to help you be your own boss:

Set your goals: Identify what you want to achieve and create a clear vision of your future. This can include your business goals, personal aspirations, and the lifestyle you want to live.

Visualize yourself in the future: Imagine yourself having already achieved your goals. Visualize yourself as a successful small business owner or entrepreneur, with all the things you want in your life.

Focus on positive feelings: When visualizing your future, focus on the positive emotions and feelings you associate with success. This can help you maintain a positive outlook and increase your motivation to take action.

Make it real: Write down your vision, create a collage or a vision board, or use other creative tools to bring your vision to life. The more you can make your vision real and tangible, the easier it will be to keep it at the forefront of your mind.

Take action: Once you have a clear vision of your future, take action to make it a reality. Break your goals down into smaller, manageable steps, and take the time to plan and execute each one.

By visualizing yourself as you want to be and taking action to make it a reality, you can increase your chances of success as a small business owner or entrepreneur. Remember, visualization is a powerful tool, but it is just one part of the process. You must also be willing to work hard and take action to achieve your goals.

Power of Written Goals

"I am always ready to learn although I do not always like being taught." — Winston Churchill

Once upon a time, there was a young man named Barry who dreamed of being his own boss. He was tired of working long hours for someone else, not having control over his schedule, and not being able to take vacations when he wanted. He had always been told that the key to success was hard work, but he had come to realize that there was more to it than that.

One day, Barry stumbled upon a book about the power of written goals. The author claimed that writing down specific, measurable, and achievable goals was the key to success, and Barry was intrigued. He had never really thought about setting goals for himself before, and he was eager to give it a try.

So, Barry sat down with a notebook and pen and began to write. He thought long and hard about what he wanted to achieve and wrote down a list of goals that he wanted to accomplish. He made sure each goal was specific, measurable, and achievable. He wrote down how he would achieve each goal, what steps he needed to take, and what resources he would need. He also wrote down a deadline for each goal, so that he could hold himself accountable.

The next day, Barry woke up with a new sense of purpose. He felt like he had a roadmap to success and he was excited to get started. He read his list of goals every day, reminding himself of what he wanted to achieve. He was amazed at how much more focused and motivated he felt, now that he had a clear direction.

As Barry began to take action, he started to see progress. He was making headway on his goals, and he felt proud of himself. He was also surprised to see that he was working harder than ever before, but he didn't feel stressed or overwhelmed. He felt energized and inspired.

A few months later, Barry was amazed at how much he had accomplished. He had met all of his goals, and he had even exceeded some of them. He realized that writing down his goals had been the key to his success. It had given him a roadmap to follow and held him accountable. He had also learned that setting goals wasn't just about working hard, but it was also about working smart.

With a new sense of confidence, Barry quit his job and started his own business. He was finally his own boss and he was proud of all that he had accomplished. He never forgot the power of written goals and he continued to set and achieve new goals every day. He had learned that the key to success was not just hard work, but it was also having a clear direction, a roadmap to follow, and the power of written goals.

And so, Barry lived happily ever after, never forgetting the power of written goals and inspiring others to do the same.

The power of written goals is an important factor to consider when you are trying to be your own boss and achieve success. Here are a few reasons why writing down your goals is so powerful:

Clarity: Writing down your goals helps you clarify what you want to achieve and why. This can help you stay focused and motivated, and ensure that you are making progress towards your vision.

Tangibility: Writing down your goals makes them more tangible and helps you to keep them front-of-mind. You can use a journal, create a vision board, or use any other method that works for you, but the key is to make sure your goals are visible and accessible.

Tracking progress: Writing down your goals allows you to track your progress and measure your success. You can see how far you've come, and identify areas where you need to improve.

Accountability: Writing down your goals makes you accountable to yourself. When you know that you have committed to a specific goal, you are more likely to take action and work towards achieving it.

Visualization: Writing down your goals helps you to visualize yourself as you want to be. This can help you stay focused and motivated, and increase your chances of success.

By taking advantage of the power of written goals, you can increase your chances of success as a small business owner or entrepreneur. Remember, the key is to be consistent and persistent in working towards your goals, and to be willing to adjust and adapt as needed.

One need to create a set of goals

Creating a set of goals is an important step towards being your own boss and achieving success. Goals help you stay focused and motivated, and provide a roadmap for your journey as a small business owner or entrepreneur.

Here are a few tips for creating a set of goals:

Start with your vision: What do you want to achieve as a small business owner or entrepreneur? Start by identifying your long-term vision, and then break it down into smaller, achievable goals.

Make your goals specific: Make sure your goals are specific and measurable. Instead of saying, "I want to grow my business," say, "I want to increase my revenue by 20% in the next six months."

Set deadlines: Give yourself a deadline for each goal. This will help you stay focused and motivated, and ensure that you are making progress towards your vision.

Prioritize your goals: Decide which goals are most important and prioritize them. Make sure to focus on the goals that will have the biggest impact on your business, and tackle them first.

Write your goals down: Writing down your goals makes them more tangible and helps you to keep them front-of-mind. You can use a journal, create a vision board, or use any other method that works for you.

Review your goals regularly: Regularly review your goals to see how you are progressing and make any necessary adjustments. This can help you stay focused and motivated, and ensure that you are making progress towards your vision.

By creating a set of goals and following these tips, you can increase your chances of success as a small business owner or entrepreneur. Remember, setting goals is just the first step. You must also take action and be willing to work hard to achieve them.

One need to set goal for everyday

Setting daily goals can be an effective way to help you achieve your larger objectives as a small business owner or entrepreneur. Here are a few tips for setting and achieving your daily goals:

Align with your long-term goals: Make sure your daily goals are aligned with your larger objectives. This will help you stay focused and motivated, and ensure that you are making progress towards your vision.

Make them achievable: Choose daily goals that are achievable and realistic. If you set goals that are too challenging, you may become discouraged and demotivated.

Keep them simple: Focus on a few key tasks each day, rather than trying to accomplish too much. This will help you stay focused and increase your chances of success.

Write them down: Write down your daily goals, so that you can keep track of your progress. This can help you stay motivated and focused, and ensure that you are making progress towards your vision.

Prioritize: Prioritize your daily goals and make sure to focus on the most important tasks first. This will help you maximize your productivity and achieve your goals more efficiently.

Reflect and adjust: At the end of each day, take a few minutes to reflect on your progress and make any necessary adjustments to your goals for the next day.

By setting daily goals and following these tips, you can increase your chances of success as a small business owner or entrepreneur. Remember, the key is to be consistent and persistent in working towards your goals, and to be willing to adjust and adapt as needed.

CHAPTER NINE

Exercise Along with The Life's Goals

"Live as if you were to die tomorrow. Learn as if you were to live forever." — Mahatma Gandhi

Once upon a time, there was a young woman named Sarah who felt unfulfilled in her job. She worked long hours for someone else, and she felt like her life was passing her by. She had always dreamt of being her own boss and having the freedom to create her own schedule, but she felt stuck.

One day, Sarah came across a motivational speaker who talked about the power of setting and achieving goals. The speaker emphasized that in order to change your life, you need to not only set goals but also review them regularly and take action towards them. Sarah was inspired, and she decided to give it a try.

She sat down with a notebook and pen and wrote down her list of goals. She made sure each goal was specific, measurable, and achievable, and she wrote down the steps she would need to take to achieve each goal. She also made a plan to review her goals regularly, to see how she was progressing and make any necessary changes.

The next day, Sarah woke up feeling like a new person. She had a newfound sense of purpose and direction. She reviewed her goals every day, and she was amazed at how much more focused and motivated she felt. She was also determined to take action towards her goals, so she decided to add exercise to her daily routine.

As Sarah started to take action, she noticed a significant change in her life. Not only was she making progress on her goals, but she was also feeling healthier and more energetic. She realized that exercise not only helped her stay physically fit but also gave her the energy and focus she needed to tackle her goals.

A few months later, Sarah was amazed at how much she had accomplished. She had met all of her goals, and she was feeling proud of herself. She had also developed a new appreciation for the power of regular exercise and the impact it had on her life.

With a new sense of confidence, Sarah quit her job and started her own business. She was finally her own boss and she was proud of all that she had accomplished. She never forgot the importance of regularly reviewing her goals and exercising, and she continued to set and achieve new goals every day.

And so, Sarah lived happily ever after, never forgetting the power of regularly reviewing her goals and exercising, and inspiring others to do the same.

Reviewing your goals and exercising regularly are two key steps to help you change your life and be your own boss. Here's how these two actions can help you achieve your goals:

Reviewing your goals: Regularly reviewing your goals can help you stay focused and motivated, and ensure that you are making progress towards your vision. This can involve re-reading your goals, checking your progress, and making any necessary adjustments to your plan.

Exercising: Regular exercise has many benefits, including improving your mental and physical health, reducing stress, and boosting your energy levels. By making exercise a regular part of your routine, you can help to improve your overall well-being and increase your chances of success.

Both of these actions, when combined, can help you make positive changes in your life and achieve your goals. Regular goal-setting and progress tracking can help you stay focused and motivated, while exercise can help you to maintain good physical and mental health, which is essential for success.

Remember, the key to success is consistency and persistence. By making goal-reviewing and exercise part of your routine, you can increase your chances of success as a small business owner or entrepreneur.

One need layout of all major goals

Laying out all of your major goals is an important step for anyone who wants to be their own boss and achieve success. Here's why:

Clarity: When you lay out your major goals, you are able to see a clear picture of what you want to achieve. This can help you to focus your efforts and prioritize your tasks.

Motivation: Seeing a clear picture of your goals can help to motivate you and keep you on track. By having a clear understanding of what you want to achieve, you are better able to stay focused and motivated.

Planning: Laying out your major goals can help you to create a plan for achieving those goals. You can identify the steps you need to take and create a timeline for each step.

Tracking progress: When you lay out your major goals, you are able to track your progress towards each one. This can help you to see what's working and what's not, and make any necessary adjustments to your plan.

Flexibility: Laying out your major goals allows you to be flexible and adjust your plans as needed. If you encounter challenges or setbacks, you can modify your approach and keep moving forward.

By laying out all of your major goals, you can gain clarity, focus, and motivation. This can help you to be successful as a small business owner or entrepreneur, and achieve the success you want in your life.

CHAPTER TEN

Plan Every Day

"Wisdom is not a product of schooling but of the lifelong attempt to acquire it." — Albert Einstein

Once upon a time, there was a young man named David who felt stuck in his job. He worked long hours for someone else and felt like he was just going through the motions. He dreamed of being his own boss, but he didn't know how to make it happen.

One day, David stumbled upon a book about the importance of planning. The author claimed that planning your day in advance was the key to success, and David was intrigued. He had never really thought about planning his day before, and he was eager to give it a try.

So, David sat down with a notebook and pen and started to plan his day. He wrote down everything he needed to do, and he made sure to prioritize his tasks based on their level of importance. He also made sure to schedule time for self-care, such as exercise and meditation, to ensure that he was taking care of himself.

The next day, David woke up with a new sense of purpose. He felt like he had a roadmap to follow, and he was excited to get started. He followed his plan throughout the day and was amazed at how much more productive he was. He was able to get more done in less time and he felt a sense of satisfaction at the end of the day.

As David continued to plan his day in advance, he started to see progress. He was making headway on his goals, and he felt proud of himself. He was also surprised to see that he was working smarter, not harder. He was able to prioritize his tasks and focus on what was important, which made him more productive and less stressed.

A few months later, David had a breakthrough. He realized that the key to success was not just hard work, but it was also about working smart. He had learned that planning his day in advance was the key to his success, and he was determined to continue doing it.

With a new sense of confidence, David quit his job and started his own business. He was finally his own boss, and he was proud of all that he had accomplished. He never forgot the importance of planning his day in advance and he continued to do so every day.

And so, David lived happily ever after, never forgetting the power of planning his day in advance, and inspiring others to do the same.

Planning your day in advance is an important habit for anyone looking to be their own boss and achieve success. Here's why:

Time management: Planning your day in advance helps you prioritize your tasks and manage your time more effectively. By knowing what you need to do and when, you can make sure that you are using your time wisely and making progress towards your goals.

Increased productivity: When you plan your day in advance, you are able to start each day with a clear idea of what you want to accomplish. This can help you to be more productive and get more done in less time.

Reduced stress: Planning your day in advance can help you to feel more in control and reduce stress. When you know what you need to do and when, you are better able to manage your workload and avoid feeling overwhelmed.

Better focus: Planning your day in advance helps you to focus on what's important and avoid distractions. You can prioritize your tasks and make sure that you are spending your time and energy on the most important things.

Improved decision-making: When you plan your day in advance, you are better able to make decisions about how to allocate your time and resources. This can help you to make more informed and effective decisions, and increase your chances of success.

By taking the time to plan your day in advance, you can increase your productivity, reduce stress, and make better use of your time. This can help you to achieve your goals and be successful as a small business owner or entrepreneur.

• 35 •

CHAPTER ELEVEN

Planning A Project

"Tell me and I forget, teach me and I may remember, involve me and I learn." — Benjamin Franklin

Once upon a time, there was a young man named Oliver who felt unfulfilled in his job. He worked long hours for someone else and felt like he was just going through the motions. He dreamed of being his own boss, but he didn't know how to make it happen.

One day, Oliver came across a business book that talked about the importance of planning a project. The author claimed that planning was the key to success, and Oliver was intrigued. He had never really thought about planning a project before, and he was eager to give it a try.

So, Oliver decided to plan a project. He sat down with a notebook and pen and started to map out the steps he would need to take to bring his project to life. He made sure to break the project down into smaller, manageable tasks, and he made a timeline for each task. He also made sure to plan for potential obstacles and how he would overcome them.

The next day, Oliver woke up feeling like a new person. He had a newfound sense of purpose and direction. He was eager to get started on his project, and he felt confident that he had a solid plan in place. He followed his plan throughout the day and was amazed at how much progress he was making. He felt like he was finally in control.

As Oliver continued to plan and execute his project, he started to see success. He was making headway on his goals, and he felt proud of himself. He was also surprised to see that he was working smarter, not harder. He was able to prioritize his tasks and focus on what was important, which made him more productive and less stressed.

A few months later, Oliver's project was a success. He had accomplished what he had set out to do, and he felt proud of himself. He realized that planning was the key to his success, and he was determined to continue doing it.

With a new sense of confidence, Oliver quit his job and started his own business. He was finally his own boss, and he was proud of all that he had accomplished. He never forgot the importance of planning a project and he continued to do so every time he embarked on a new project.

And so, Oliver lived happily ever after, never forgetting the power of planning a project, and inspiring others to do the same.

Planning a project is an important step for anyone who wants to be their own boss and achieve success. Here are some key steps to help you plan a project effectively:

Define the project: Start by defining the project and understanding its goals and objectives. Consider what you want to achieve and what you need to do to get there.

Identify resources: Next, identify the resources you will need to complete the project. This may include people, materials, equipment, and funding.

Create a timeline: Create a timeline for the project, including the start and end dates and any important milestones along the way. Make sure to build in time for any unexpected events or changes.

Assign tasks: Assign specific tasks to team members, and make sure everyone knows what they are responsible for. Delegate tasks based on individual strengths and skills.

Monitor progress: Monitor progress regularly and make any necessary adjustments to the plan. Be flexible and adaptable, and be prepared to make changes if needed.

Evaluate and adjust: After the project is complete, evaluate the results and make any necessary adjustments. Consider what you did well, what could have been done better, and what you can learn from the experience.

By planning a project effectively, you can ensure that you are using your resources effectively, and that you are able to complete the project on time and within budget. This can help you to be successful as a small business owner or entrepreneur and achieve the success you want in your life.

CHAPTER TWELVE

Execute The List of Different Purposes

"True teachers are those who use themselves as bridges over which they invite their students to cross; then, having facilitated their crossing, joyfully collapse, encouraging them to create their own." — Nikos Kazantzakis

Once upon a time, there was a young woman named Sarah who felt trapped in her job. She worked long hours for someone else and felt like she was just going through the motions. She dreamed of being her own boss, but she didn't know how to make it happen.

One day, Sarah stumbled upon a book about the importance of having a list of different purposes. The author claimed that having a list of purposes was the key to success, and Sarah was intrigued. She had never really thought about having a list of purposes before, and she was eager to give it a try.

So, Sarah sat down with a notebook and pen and started to write down her different purposes. She wrote down everything she wanted to accomplish, both professionally and personally. She made sure to prioritize her purposes based on their level of importance, and she made a plan to execute each one.

The next day, Sarah woke up with a new sense of purpose. She felt like she had a roadmap to follow, and she was excited to get started. She followed her plan throughout the day and was amazed at how much more productive she was. She was able to get more done in less time and she felt a sense of satisfaction at the end of the day.

As Sarah continued to execute her purposes, she started to see progress. She was making headway on her goals, and she felt proud of herself. She was also surprised to see that she was working smarter, not harder. She was able to prioritize her tasks and focus on what was important, which made her more productive and less stressed.

A few months later, Sarah had a breakthrough. She realized that the key to success was not just hard work, but it was also about working smart. She had learned that having a list of different purposes was the key to her success, and she was determined to continue doing it.

With a new sense of confidence, Sarah quit her job and started her own business. She was finally her own boss, and she was proud of all that she had accomplished. She never forgot the importance of having a list of different purposes and she continued to do so every day.

And so, Sarah lived happily ever after, never forgetting the power of having a list of different purposes, and inspiring others to do the same.

Having a list of different purposes and executing them is an important step for anyone who wants to be their own boss and achieve success. Here's why:

Clarity: When you have a list of different purposes, you are able to see a clear picture of what you want to achieve. This can help you to focus your efforts and prioritize your tasks.

Motivation: Seeing a clear list of your purposes can help to motivate you and keep you on track. By having a clear understanding of what you want to achieve, you are better able to stay focused and motivated.

Planning: Having a list of purposes can help you to create a plan for achieving those goals. You can identify the steps you need to take and create a timeline for each step.

Tracking progress: When you have a list of purposes, you are able to track your progress towards each one. This can help you to see what's working and what's not, and make any necessary adjustments to your plan.

Flexibility: Having a list of purposes allows you to be flexible and adjust your plans as needed. If you encounter challenges or setbacks, you can modify your approach and keep moving forward.

By having a list of different purposes and executing them, you can gain clarity, focus, and motivation. This can help you to be successful as a small business owner or entrepreneur, and achieve the success you want in your life.

CHAPTER THIRTEEN

Apply The 80/20 Rule

"Anyone who stops learning is old, whether at 20 or 80. Anyone who keeps learning stays young. The greatest thing in life is to keep your mind young." — Henry Ford

Once upon a time, there was a young man named David who felt stuck in his job. He worked long hours for someone else and felt like he was just going through the motions. He dreamed of being his own boss, but he didn't know how to make it happen.

One day, David heard about the Pareto Principal, also known as the 80/20 rule. The idea behind the Pareto Principal is that 80% of the results come from 20% of the efforts. David was intrigued and decided to try to apply the Pareto Principal to everything he did.

So, David started to focus on the 20% of his tasks that were bringing him the most results. He made a list of these tasks and made sure to prioritize them. He also made a plan to delegate or eliminate the tasks that were bringing him the least results.

The next day, David woke up with a new sense of purpose. He felt like he had a roadmap to follow, and he was excited to get started. He followed his plan throughout the day and was amazed at how much more productive he was. He was able to get more done in less time and he felt a sense of satisfaction at the end of the day.

As David continued to apply the Pareto Principal, he started to see progress. He was making headway on his goals, and he felt proud of himself. He was also surprised to see that he was working smarter, not harder. He was able to prioritize his tasks and focus on what was important, which made him more productive and less stressed.

A few months later, David had a breakthrough. He realized that the key to success was not just hard work, but it was also about working smart. He had learned that the Pareto Principal was the key to his success, and he was determined to continue doing it.

With a new sense of confidence, David quit his job and started his own business. He was finally his own boss, and he was proud of all that he had accomplished. He never forgot the importance of applying the Pareto Principal to everything he did, and he continued to do so every day.

And so, David lived happily ever after, never forgetting the power of the Pareto Principal, and inspiring others to do the same.

The Pareto Principle, also known as the 80/20 rule, is a useful tool for anyone who wants to be their own boss and achieve success. The principle states that roughly 80% of results come from 20% of the effort.

Here's how you can apply the Pareto Principle to your business:

Identify the 20%: Focus on the 20% of your tasks or activities that will produce 80% of your results. This can help you to prioritize your efforts and focus on what's really important.

Delegate or eliminate: Consider delegating or eliminating the tasks that are low-value or that don't contribute to your goals. This can free up your time and allow you to focus on the tasks that really matter.

Focus on high-impact activities: Spend your time on high-impact activities that will move you closer to your goals. This can help you to maximize your results and achieve more in less time.

Monitor progress: Regularly monitor your progress and measure the impact of your efforts. This can help you to see what's working and what's not, and make any necessary adjustments.

By applying the Pareto Principle to everything, you can be more productive, effective, and successful as a small business owner or entrepreneur. This can help you to achieve your goals and reach new levels of success.

CHAPTER FOURTEEN

Focus On Activities Not Accomplishments

"There is divine beauty in learning.... To learn means to accept the postulate that life did not begin at my birth. Others have been here before me, and I walk in their footsteps." — Elie Wiesel

Once upon a time, there was a young man named Peter who dreamed of being his own boss. He had always been fascinated by the idea of having the freedom to make his own decisions, chart his own course and be in control of his own success. He was driven to succeed and was determined to make his dream a reality.

One day, Peter decided to quit his job and start his own business. He was filled with excitement and passion, eager to make a difference in the world. He began to focus on accomplishing as much as he could in the shortest amount of time. He worked tirelessly, putting in long hours and sacrificing his personal life for the sake of his business.

But as time went on, Peter began to realize that his approach was not sustainable. He was exhausted and burnt out, and his business was not growing as quickly as he had hoped. He was constantly stressed and felt like a failure.

One day, a wise old man approached Peter and offered him some advice. He told Peter that the key to being a successful business owner was not to focus on accomplishing as much as possible, but rather to focus on the activities that would lead to success. The old man explained that success was not about how much you accomplished, but rather about how much you enjoyed the journey.

Peter took the old man's advice to heart and decided to make a change. He slowed down and focused on the activities that he enjoyed, such as networking and building relationships with customers and suppliers. He also made time for self-care and to pursue his hobbies and interests.

To Peter's surprise, his business started to thrive. He was no longer burnt out and exhausted, and his customers and employees could sense his newfound energy and passion. He was able to strike a balance between work and life, and was finally happy and fulfilled.

Peter learned that being your own boss is not just about accomplishing as much as possible, but rather about finding joy in the journey and doing what you love. He was proud of himself for having the courage to take the road less traveled and for making his dream a reality.

From that day forward, Peter lived a life filled with purpose and happiness, always striving to focus on the activities that brought him joy and success. And so, he became known as one of the most successful and respected business owners in the community, all because he learned the value of focusing on activities, not just accomplishments.

Focusing on activities rather than accomplishments is a key aspect of being your own boss and achieving success. Here's why:

Consistency: Focusing on activities helps you to maintain a consistent effort towards your goals. Rather than getting caught up in the outcome, you can focus on the actions you need to take to achieve those outcomes.

Process-oriented mind-set: Focusing on activities helps you to adopt a process-oriented mind-set, rather than a results-oriented one. This can help you to stay motivated and focused, even when results are slow to come.

Flexibility: By focusing on activities, you are able to be flexible and adjust your approach as needed. If you encounter challenges or setbacks, you can modify your plan and keep moving forward.

Success-building habits: Focusing on activities helps you to develop success-building habits. By taking consistent action, you can build the habits and skills you need to achieve your goals.

By focusing on activities rather than accomplishments, you can adopt a process-oriented mind-set and maintain a consistent effort towards your goals. This can help you to be successful as a small business owner or entrepreneur, and achieve the success you want in your life.

CHAPTER FIFTEEN

Think and Feel Yourself Motivated

"Curiosity is the wick in the candle of learning." — William Arthur Ward

Once upon a time, there was a young man named Alex who worked as a software engineer in a big tech company. He was good at his job and was well-liked by his colleagues, but deep down, he felt unfulfilled. He longed to be his own boss, to work on his own terms and make a real impact on the world.

One day, Alex came across a quote that changed his life forever: "To be your own boss, one must think and feel oneself motivated." This quote resonated with him, and he began to see his life in a whole new light. He realized that he was not just a software engineer, but a creative and driven person who could make a real difference.

Alex started reading books about entrepreneurship and seeking out advice from successful business owners. He discovered that the key to being a successful entrepreneur was to believe in oneself and to have the drive and motivation to make one's dreams a reality. He also learned that success wasn't just about having a good idea, but also about having the determination and persistence to see it through.

With newfound motivation and inspiration, Alex quit his job and started working on his own software project. He worked long hours, often late into the night, driven by his passion and a strong desire to succeed. Over time, his software gained traction, and he soon had a thriving business on his hands.

Alex never looked back. He was proud of what he had accomplished, and he felt fulfilled in a way that he had never experienced before. He had become his own boss, and he loved every minute of it.

Years went by, and Alex's business continued to grow and thrive. He became known as a successful entrepreneur and was sought after for his wisdom and advice. But he never forgot the quote that had inspired him to pursue his dreams in the first place, and he often repeated it to others who sought to follow in his footsteps.

"To be your own boss, one must think and feel oneself motivated," he would say. "Believe in yourself, and the rest will follow."

And so, Alex's story became a testament to the power of motivation and the importance of following one's dreams. He proved that with determination and hard work, anyone can be their own boss and achieve success on their own terms.

Thinking and feeling motivated is a critical aspect of being your own boss and achieving success. Here's why:

Positive mind-set: By thinking and feeling motivated, you can adopt a positive mind-set that is conducive to success. This can help you to stay focused and energized, even when faced with challenges and obstacles.

Goal-oriented behavior: Thinking and feeling motivated can help you to maintain goal-oriented behavior. You'll be more likely to take the actions you need to take to achieve your goals, and less likely to be side tracked by distractions or negativity.

Increased productivity: When you think and feel motivated, you are likely to be more productive and effective. You'll have more energy, focus, and drive, and will be better equipped to tackle the tasks and challenges of running your own business.

Improved decision-making: Thinking and feeling motivated can also improve your decision-making skills. You'll be more confident, decisive, and proactive, and will be better equipped to make the right decisions for your business.

By thinking and feeling motivated, you can adopt a positive mind-set and maintain goal-oriented behavior. This can help you to be successful as a small business owner or entrepreneur, and achieve the success you want in your life.

CHAPTER SIXTEEN

Good Time Management Makes Better Decisions

"Education is the ability to listen to almost anything without losing your temper or your self-confidence." — Robert Frost

Once upon a time, there was a young woman named Sarah who worked as a project manager in a marketing firm. She was skilled at her job and was highly valued by her boss, but she felt unfulfilled. She dreamed of being her own boss, to run her own business and make a real impact on the world.

One day, Sarah came across a quote that changed her life forever: "To be your own boss, one must know good time management and make better decisions." This quote resonated with her, and she began to see her life in a whole new light. She realized that she was not just a project manager, but a driven and ambitious person who had the potential to make a real difference.

Sarah started to study the art of time management and decision-making, and she quickly discovered that these skills were essential for success as an entrepreneur. She learned that good time management meant prioritizing tasks, setting achievable goals, and being efficient with her time. She also learned that making good decisions required being able to weigh the pros and cons of different options and taking calculated risks when necessary.

With her newfound knowledge and confidence, Sarah quit her job and started her own marketing firm. She threw herself into the business, working tirelessly to build her client base and establish her brand. Despite the long hours and the many challenges, she faced, Sarah remained focused and determined. She knew that success as a business owner depended on her ability to manage her time and make good decisions.

Over time, Sarah's business grew and flourished. She became known for her excellent time management skills and her ability to make sound decisions. Her clients were impressed by her efficiency and her commitment to their success, and her business became one of the most sought-after marketing firms in the city.

Years went by, and Sarah's business continued to thrive. She was proud of what she had accomplished and grateful for the opportunities that had come her way. But she never forgot the quote that had inspired her to pursue her dreams in the first place, and she often repeated it to others who sought to follow in her footsteps.

"To be your own boss, one must know good time management and make better decisions," she would say. "It takes hard work, focus, and determination, but the rewards are worth it."

And so, Sarah's story became a testament to the power of good time management and the importance of making good decisions. She proved that with the right skills and a strong work ethic, anyone can be their own boss and achieve success on their own terms.

Good time management and making better decisions are critical components of being your own boss and achieving success. Here's why:

Increased productivity: Good time management helps you to be more productive and effective. By prioritizing your tasks and focusing on the most important ones, you can ensure that you are using your time and energy wisely.

Improved decision-making: Good time management also helps you to make better decisions. When you are not overwhelmed by a long to-do list and have the mental space to think clearly, you'll be better equipped to make the right decisions for your business.

Better work-life balance: Good time management can also help you to achieve a better work-life balance. By prioritizing your time and energy, you can ensure that you are able to spend time on the things that matter most, both in your personal and professional life.

Reduced stress and burnout: By managing your time effectively, you can also reduce stress and burnout. When you are not constantly feeling rushed or overwhelmed, you'll be able to work more efficiently and enjoy your life more fully.

Good time management and making better decisions are key skills for anyone looking to be their own boss and achieve success. By focusing on these areas, you can be more productive, make better decisions, and achieve the success you want in your life.

CHAPTER SEVENTEEN

Be A Long Term Super Critical Thinker

"Learning is not attained by chance. It must be sought for with ardour and attended with diligence." — Abigail Adams

Once upon a time, there was a young man named Francis who was tired of working for someone else. He dreamed of being his own boss, of being in charge of his own destiny, and of having the freedom to make his own choices. But he knew that this was not going to be easy. The road to success was long, and he would have to be a critical thinker if he was going to make it to the top.

Francis was determined to make his dream a reality, so he started reading books about business, finance, and entrepreneurship. He learned about the importance of long-term planning and the dangers of short-term thinking. He also discovered that success was not just about making money, but about making a difference in the world. He began to see himself as a leader, a visionary, and a problem solver.

With this newfound knowledge, Francis decided to start his own business. He started small, with just a few clients and a single product, but he never lost sight of his long-term goals. He was always thinking ahead, always considering the future and the impact that his decisions would have. He was a critical thinker, always looking for ways to improve his business, his products, and himself.

As his business grew, Francis encountered many challenges and obstacles, but he never lost his focus. He was always looking for ways to overcome these obstacles and to find new opportunities. He was always looking for ways to stay ahead of the competition and to be the best in his field.

Years passed, and Francis's business became a success. He had employees, a loyal customer base, and a reputation for excellence. He was proud of what he had achieved, but he never lost sight of his long-term goals. He continued to be a critical thinker, always looking for ways to improve and to make a difference in the world.

In the end, Francis's success was not just about making money, but about making a difference in the world. He had become his own boss, and he had proven that with hard work, determination, and critical thinking, anyone can achieve their dreams.

The moral of the story is that to be your own boss, one needs to be a long-term critical superior thinker. With a clear vision and a strategic plan, anything is possible. So, if you have a dream, don't give up on it. Keep pushing forward, always be critical, and never stop thinking about the future. You too can be your own boss and make a difference in the world.

Being a superior thinker is an important aspect of being your own boss and achieving success. Here's why:

Problem-solving skills: Superior thinking helps you to solve problems more effectively. As a business owner, you will face a wide range of challenges, and being able to think critically and creatively can help you to overcome these obstacles.

Strategic thinking: Superior thinking also enables you to think strategically. You'll be able to see the big picture and make the right decisions for your business, rather than getting bogged down in the details.

Better decision-making: Superior thinking also helps you to make better decisions. You'll be more confident, decisive, and proactive, and will be better equipped to make the right decisions for your business.

Improved communication skills: Superior thinking can also help you to communicate more effectively. You'll be able to articulate your thoughts and ideas more clearly, and will be better able to persuade and influence others.

By developing your thinking skills and becoming a superior thinker, you'll be better equipped to handle the challenges of being your own boss and achieve success in your life. This can include reading and learning about different approaches to thinking and problem-solving, practicing critical and creative thinking, and seeking feedback from others to help you improve your skills.

Being a critical thinker is a crucial component of being your own boss and achieving success. Here's why:

Problem-solving skills: Critical thinking helps you to solve problems more effectively. As a business owner, you will face a wide range of challenges, and being able to think critically can help you to overcome these obstacles.

Improved decision-making: Critical thinking also enables you to make better decisions. You'll be able to evaluate information and options more objectively, and will be better equipped to make informed decisions for your business.

Better communication skills: Critical thinking can also help you to communicate more effectively. You'll be able to articulate your thoughts and ideas more clearly, and will be better able to persuade and influence others.

Increased creativity: Critical thinking can also enhance your creativity. By questioning assumptions and exploring new ideas, you'll be better able to develop innovative solutions for your business.

By developing your critical thinking skills, you'll be better equipped to handle the challenges of being your own boss and achieve success in your life. This can include reading and learning about different approaches to critical thinking, practicing critical thinking exercises, and seeking feedback from others to help you improve your skills.

Owning a Business: Plan goals and plan accordingly. Being your own boss means taking complete responsibility for the success or failure of your business. It requires careful planning, financial management, and the ability to handle both the highs and lows of running a business.

It's important to have a clear vision of what you want to achieve and a solid plan in place to get there. This may involve researching your market, developing a business plan, securing funding, and building a team of employees or partners to help you reach your goals.

Additionally, as a business owner, you'll need to be self-disciplined, motivated, and able to make tough decisions. You'll also need to be able to adapt to change and be willing to take calculated risks.

But the rewards of being your own boss can be significant, including having control over your work schedule, the ability to pursue your passion, and the potential to earn a higher income. If you're willing to put in the hard work and make the necessary sacrifices, starting and running a successful business can be a highly fulfilling and rewarding experience.

CHAPTER EIGHTEEN

The Law of Forced Efficiency

"Being a student is easy. Learning requires actual work." —
William Crawford

Once upon a time, there was a young man named Clinton who always dreamed of starting his own business. He was ambitious, hardworking, and eager to make a difference in the world. However, despite his best efforts, he never seemed to get ahead. He was stuck in a dead-end job, working long hours for someone else's dreams, and barely making enough money to make ends meet.

One day, Clinton finally decided that he had enough. He was going to be his own boss, no matter what it took. He quit his job, sold his car, and used the money to start a small business selling handmade crafts.

At first, everything was going great. Clinton was his own boss, he made his own schedule, and he was finally able to turn his dreams into a reality. But soon, he realized that being an entrepreneur was much harder than he thought. He was working even longer hours, spending more money than he was making, and constantly struggling to keep up with the demands of running a business.

That's when Clinton discovered the law of forced efficiency. He learned that in order to be truly successful, he needed to work smarter, not harder. He needed to find ways to maximize his productivity, minimize his expenses, and streamline his operations. He started reading books on entrepreneurship, attending workshops and seminars, and reaching out to other successful business owners for advice.

With each passing day, Clinton's business grew stronger. He was able to find new and innovative ways to increase his efficiency, and as a result, he was able to increase his profits and grow his business. He was no longer just surviving, he was thriving.

Years went by, and Clinton's business became a huge success. He was recognized as one of the top entrepreneurs in the country, and he was able to provide a comfortable life for himself and his family. He never forgot the lessons he learned along the way, and he was always grateful for the law of forced efficiency.

In the end, Clinton proved that anyone can be their own boss, as long as they are willing to obey the law of forced efficiency. He showed that with hard work, determination, and a willingness to learn, anyone can turn their dreams into a reality.

Yes, obeying the law of forced efficiency is an important aspect of being your own boss. The law of forced efficiency states that in order to be successful as an entrepreneur, you need to continually improve your processes and find ways to do more with less.

This means being mindful of the time and resources you have available, and making the most of them. For example, you may need to automate certain tasks, delegate responsibilities, or find more efficient methods for achieving your goals.

Additionally, it's important to stay focused on your core competencies and prioritize the tasks that will have the biggest impact on your business. This may mean saying no to certain projects or opportunities that don't align with your goals, and focusing on what you do best.

Ultimately, the key to success as a business owner is to be strategic, resourceful, and efficient. By following the law of forced efficiency, you can ensure that your efforts are focused where they will have the most impact.

One need to work on maximum productivity

Yes, working on maximum productivity is critical to success as your own boss. As a business owner, you wear many hats and are responsible for a wide range of tasks, so it's important to be efficient and productive with your time.

Here are a few tips to help you increase your productivity:

Set clear goals and priorities: Having a clear idea of what you want to achieve and what's most important will help you stay focused and avoid getting bogged down in unimportant tasks.

Use time-management tools: Tools like calendars, to-do lists, and productivity apps can help you keep track of your tasks and schedule, and ensure you're using your time effectively.

Minimize distractions: Distractions can be a major productivity killer. Find ways to minimize distractions in your work environment, such as closing your office door, using noise-cancelling headphones, or turning off notifications on your phone.

Take breaks: Taking breaks can help you avoid burnout and increase your focus and productivity. Try to take regular breaks throughout the day, even if it's just for a few minutes at a time.

Delegate tasks: As a business owner, it's important to delegate tasks to others when possible. This can help you free up time to focus on more important tasks, and also allow others to grow and develop their skills.

By working on maximum productivity, you can ensure that you are making the most of your time and resources, and that you are able to achieve your goals as a business owner.

CHAPTER NINETEEN

Manage to Work Under Pressure of Deadline

"If you think education is expensive, try estimating the cost of ignorance." — Howard Gardner

Once upon a time, there was a young man named Banner who was tired of working for someone else. He dreamt of starting his own business and becoming his own boss. He had always been an ambitious and hardworking individual, but he was often frustrated by the pressure of deadlines imposed by his bosses. Banner felt that he could do better on his own, without the constraints of working for someone else.

One day, Banner finally mustered up the courage to quit his job and start his own company. He was determined to create a business that was driven by passion and creativity, rather than the pressure of deadlines. He was determined to prove to himself and to the world that success could be achieved without being confined by time constraints.

At first, Banner struggled to adapt to the freedom that came with being his own boss. He found it difficult to manage his time and to stay focused on his goals. But he quickly learned that the key to success was to set realistic and achievable deadlines for himself, and to work diligently towards them. He also realized that it was important to take breaks and to recharge, in order to maintain his focus and creativity.

As Banner's business started to grow, he found that he was able to create something truly special. He was able to offer a unique product or service that was driven by his passion and creativity, and that was not limited by the constraints of working for someone else. Customers were drawn to his business, not only because of the quality of his work, but also because of the energy and excitement that he brought to his work.

Eventually, Banner's business became one of the most successful and well-respected companies in his industry. People marveled at how he was able to achieve so much without being driven by the pressure of deadlines. Banner was proud of what he had accomplished, and he was grateful for the freedom that came with being his own boss.

In the end, Banner realized that success comes from within, and that it is not dependent on the pressure of deadlines imposed by others. He learned that one can achieve great things by simply staying focused on their goals, and by working hard towards them. He also learned that one can be truly successful and fulfilled, by simply being true to themselves and following their passions. And so, Banner lived happily ever after, as his own boss, and as a true master of his own destiny.

It's true that one should try to avoid working under pressure of deadlines as much as possible. When you're constantly working under tight deadlines, it can lead to stress, burnout, and decreased productivity.

Here are a few tips to help you avoid work under pressure of deadlines:

Plan ahead: Anticipating deadlines and creating a plan to meet them can help you avoid last-minute rushes and the pressure that comes with them.

Prioritize tasks: Determine which tasks are most important and prioritize them accordingly. This will help you focus on what's most critical and avoid feeling overwhelmed by a long to-do list.

Break projects into smaller tasks: Breaking down larger projects into smaller, manageable tasks can help you make steady progress and avoid feeling overwhelmed.

Set realistic deadlines: Be realistic about how long it will take to complete tasks and set deadlines accordingly. This will help you avoid overcommitting and the pressure of tight deadlines.

Ask for help: Don't be afraid to reach out for help when you need it. Whether it's delegating tasks to others or seeking assistance from a mentor, asking for help can reduce your workload and relieve pressure.

By avoiding work under pressure of deadlines, you can maintain a healthy work-life balance, reduce stress, and increase your overall productivity and success as a business owner.

CHAPTER TWENTY

Practice Creative Procrastination

"I realized that becoming a master of karate was not about learning 4,000 moves but about doing just a handful of moves 4,000 times." — Chet Holmes

Once upon a time, there was a young man named Jonathan who lived in a small village. Jonathan was an aspiring entrepreneur with a burning desire to start his own business. He was tired of working for others and yearned for the freedom and autonomy that comes with being one's own boss.

However, Jonathan faced a common dilemma. He was a master of procrastination and found himself constantly putting off the tasks he needed to do in order to start his business. He struggled with finding the motivation to get started, and often found himself distracted by other activities.

One day, Jonathan met an old sage who lived in the nearby mountains. The sage was renowned for his wisdom and was known to offer wise counsel to those who sought it. Jonathan approached the sage, seeking guidance on how to overcome his procrastination and finally become his own boss.

The sage listened attentively to Jonathan's story and then offered him some sage advice. "Jonathan," he said, "to be your own boss, one needs to practice creative procrastination."

Jonathan was taken aback. "Creative procrastination?" he asked. "What does that mean?"

"It means," replied the sage, "that you must find a way to harness the power of your procrastination and use it to your advantage. Instead of putting off the important tasks that will help you achieve your goal, use that time to cultivate your creativity. Read books, watch documentaries, attend workshops and seminars, and do anything that will help you generate new ideas and expand your knowledge."

Jonathan was inspired by the sage's words and decided to put his advice into action. He started to spend the time he would have spent procrastinating on creative activities that would help him grow as an entrepreneur. He read books on business and marketing, attended workshops on creativity, and watched documentaries on successful entrepreneurs.

As a result of his efforts, Jonathan's creativity flourished, and he began to see the world in a new light. He came up with innovative ideas for his business and was finally able to turn his dream of being his own boss into a reality.

Years went by, and Jonathan's business grew into a thriving enterprise. He became known as one of the most creative and successful entrepreneurs in the land, and his story inspired countless others to follow in his footsteps.

And so, the moral of the story is that to be your own boss, one must practice creative procrastination. By harnessing the power of procrastination and using it to fuel one's creativity, anything is possible.

Practicing creative procrastination can be an effective strategy for some entrepreneurs, but it's important to understand what it means and how to do it correctly.

Creative procrastination is the practice of putting off tasks that aren't urgent or important in order to focus on tasks that are more important or that require more creativity. This can help you avoid feeling overwhelmed, improve your focus, and increase your overall productivity.

However, it's important to avoid using creative procrastination as an excuse for simply avoiding tasks that you don't want to do.

Instead, you should approach it as a strategic way to prioritize your time and focus on the tasks that will have the greatest impact on your business.

Here are a few tips to help you practice creative procrastination effectively:

Prioritize tasks: Determine which tasks are most important and prioritize them accordingly. This will help you focus on what's most critical and avoid feeling overwhelmed.

Set clear goals and deadlines: Having a clear idea of what you want to achieve and when you want to achieve it will help you stay focused and motivated.

Avoid distractions: Minimize distractions that can prevent you from focusing on the task at hand.

Take breaks: Taking breaks can help you avoid burnout and increase your focus and productivity.

Reflect on your progress: Regularly reflect on your progress and assess whether you're using your time effectively. Make adjustments as necessary to ensure that you're focusing on the tasks that are most important.

By practicing creative procrastination correctly, you can improve your focus, increase your productivity, and achieve your goals as a business owner.

One need to understand procrastinate on purpose

Yes, it's important for business owners to understand the concept of "procrastinating on purpose." This means intentionally delaying certain tasks in order to focus on more important or urgent tasks.

Procrastinating on purpose can help you make better use of your time and resources, and ensure that you are focusing on the tasks that will have the greatest impact on your business.

However, it's important to avoid using procrastination as an excuse for simply avoiding tasks that you don't want to do. Instead, you should approach it as a strategic way to prioritize your time and focus on the tasks that will have the greatest impact on your business.

Here are a few tips to help you procrastinate on purpose effectively:

Prioritize tasks: Determine which tasks are most important and prioritize them accordingly. This will help you focus on what's most critical and avoid feeling overwhelmed.

Set clear goals and deadlines: Having a clear idea of what you want to achieve and when you want to achieve it will help you stay focused and motivated.

Avoid distractions: Minimize distractions that can prevent you from focusing on the task at hand.

Take breaks: Taking breaks can help you avoid burnout and increase your focus and productivity.

Reflect on your progress: Regularly reflect on your progress and assess whether you're using your time effectively. Make adjustments as necessary to ensure that you're focusing on the tasks that are most important.

By procrastinating on purpose correctly, you can improve your focus, increase your productivity, and achieve your goals as a business owner.

CHAPTER TWENTY-ONE

Priorities Versus Posteriorties

"The key to pursuing excellence is to embrace an organic, long-term learning process, and not to live in a shell of static, safe mediocrity. Usually, growth comes at the expense of previous comfort or safety." — Josh Waitzkin

Once upon a time, there was a young man named Max who dreamed of starting his own business. He was tired of the daily grind of working for someone else and longed for the freedom that came with being his own boss.

One day, Max decided to take the plunge and start his own company. He was filled with excitement and energy, eager to make his dreams a reality. However, as the days passed, Max quickly realized that running a business was not as easy as he had thought.

Max found himself pulled in a million different directions, with too many tasks to handle and not enough hours in the day. He soon discovered that the key to success was to understand the difference between priorities and posteriorties.

Priorities were the tasks that were crucial to the success of the business and needed to be completed first, while posteriorties were the less important tasks that could wait until later. Max realized that if he focused too much on the posteriorties, he would never get to the priorities and his business would suffer.

Max began to prioritize his tasks and was amazed at the results. He was able to complete important projects faster, and his business started to grow and flourish. He learned that being his own boss was not about working harder, but about working smarter.

With time, Max's business became a huge success, and he was finally able to achieve the financial freedom and independence he had always dreamed of. He was proud of what he had accomplished and grateful for the lessons he had learned along the way.

Max's story teaches us that to be our own boss, we need to understand the difference between priorities and posteriorties. By focusing on what is truly important and letting go of the rest, we can achieve great things and live a fulfilling life.

Yes, setting priorities is a key aspect of being your own boss. When you're running your own business, there are often many tasks and responsibilities competing for your time and attention. It's essential to be able to prioritize these tasks and focus your efforts on the most important ones. This requires a clear understanding of your goals and objectives and what is most critical for your business's success.

By setting priorities, you can ensure that you're using your time and resources effectively and efficiently. It also helps you stay focused and avoid getting bogged down by distractions and unimportant tasks. Additionally, by prioritizing your tasks, you can ensure that you are making progress towards your goals and achieving the outcomes you want for your business.

Prioritizing your tasks also involves setting realistic deadlines and taking the necessary steps to meet them. This means breaking down larger tasks into smaller, more manageable steps and making sure you have the resources and support you need to complete each step. By setting priorities and meeting deadlines, you can demonstrate to yourself and others that you are committed to your business and its success.

Yes, understanding the difference between priorities and posterities is critical to success as a business owner.

Priorities are tasks or responsibilities that are most important and need to be completed first. These are the tasks that have the greatest impact on your business and should take priority over other tasks.

Posterities, on the other hand, are tasks or responsibilities that can be postponed or delegated to others. These tasks may not be as urgent or important, but still need to be done at some point.

Understanding the difference between priorities and posterities can help you make better use of your time and resources, and ensure that you are focusing on the tasks that will have the greatest impact on your business.

Here are a few tips to help you prioritize your tasks:

Create a to-do list: Write down all of your tasks, both priority and posterity, so that you have a clear understanding of what needs to be done.

Assess the impact of each task: Consider how each task will impact your business and prioritize the tasks that will have the greatest impact.

Set deadlines: Establish deadlines for each task to help you stay focused and motivated.

Delegate tasks: Delegate posterity tasks to others when possible to free up time for more important tasks.

By understanding the difference between priorities and posterities, you can make the most of your time and resources and achieve your goals as a business owner.

One need to understand set posteriorties on time consuming activities

Once upon a time, there was a young man named Jonathan who had always dreamed of starting his own business. He was tired of working long hours at his corporate job, where he felt unappreciated and undervalued. Jonathan had always been a creative and entrepreneurial person, and he felt that he had a lot to offer the world. So, he made the brave decision to quit his job and start his own business.

At first, Jonathan was thrilled with the freedom that came with being his own boss. He could work on his own terms and set his own schedule. But as time went on, he quickly realized that there was a major problem with his new lifestyle: he was having trouble managing his time effectively. He found himself working longer hours than ever before, and he was constantly feeling overwhelmed and stressed out.

One day, Jonathan had a breakthrough. He realized that the key to being his own boss was to understand the importance of setting priorities. He realized that if he was going to succeed in his business, he needed to be able to prioritize the tasks that were most important and give them the time and attention they needed. He also needed to be able to say "no" to the things that were not as important, or that were simply taking up too much of his time.

With this new understanding, Jonathan started to make some changes. He made a list of all the things he needed to do for his business, and then he ranked them in order of importance. He started to allocate his time more effectively, giving the most important tasks the most time and attention. He also made a conscious effort to eliminate time-wasting activities, such as checking his email too often or getting caught up in unimportant details.

As Jonathan continued to prioritize his time and manage his workload more effectively, he started to see some amazing results. His business began to grow, and he was able to achieve more in less time. He was also less stressed and more satisfied with his work. He was finally able to enjoy the freedom and independence that came with being his own boss.

The moral of the story is that to be your own boss, one must understand the importance of setting priorities on time-consuming activities. By doing so, you can achieve greater success, reduce stress, and enjoy the freedom that comes with running your own business.

Yes, it's important for business owners to understand the concept of setting priorities on time-consuming activities. This means intentionally prioritizing the most important and impactful tasks, and putting less important tasks on the back burner.

By focusing on the most important tasks, you can make better use of your time and resources, and ensure that you are doing the work that will have the greatest impact on your business.

Here are a few tips to help you set priorities on time-consuming activities:

Identify your priorities: Determine which tasks are most important and impactful, and prioritize these tasks first.

Assess the value of each task: Consider the potential impact of each task on your business and prioritize tasks that will have the greatest impact.

Set clear goals and deadlines: Having a clear idea of what you want to achieve and when you want to achieve it will help you stay focused and motivated.

Minimize distractions: Avoid distractions that can prevent you from focusing on the task at hand.

Delegate tasks: Delegate less important tasks to others when possible to free up time for more important tasks.

By setting priorities on time-consuming activities, you can make the most of your time and resources, and achieve your goals as a business owner.

CHAPTER TWENTY-TWO

Shoulds Versus Musts

"The beautiful thing about learning is that nobody can take it away from you." — B.B. King

Once upon a time, there was a woman named Sarah who had always dreamed of starting her own business. She was tired of working for someone else and felt that she had a unique talent that the world needed to see. So, she took the leap and quit her job to start her own business as a freelance graphic designer.

At first, Sarah was thrilled with the newfound freedom that came with being her own boss. She loved the flexibility and creativity that came with working for herself. But as time went on, she started to feel overwhelmed and stressed out. She was working long hours, and she was never able to get ahead.

One day, Sarah had an epiphany. She realized that the key to being her own boss was to understand the difference between "shoulds" and "musts". She realized that there were a lot of things that she thought she "should" be doing for her business, but that were not actually necessary for its success. And there were a lot of things that she felt she "must" do, but that were actually holding her back.

With this new understanding, Sarah started to make some changes. She made a list of all the things she thought she "should" be doing for her business, and then she ranked them in order of importance. She realized that many of the things she thought she "should" be doing were not actually necessary, and that she could eliminate them from her to-do list. She also started to focus more on the things she "must" do, and to give those tasks the time and attention they deserved.

As Sarah continued to prioritize her time and focus on the things that were truly important, she started to see some amazing results. Her business began to grow, and she was able to achieve more in less time. She was also less stressed and more satisfied with her work. She was finally able to enjoy the freedom and independence that came with being her own boss.

The moral of the story is that to be your own boss, one must understand the difference between "shoulds" and "musts". By focusing on the things that are truly important, and eliminating the things that are not, you can achieve greater success, reduce stress, and enjoy the freedom that comes with running your own business.

Yes, that's true. When starting your own business, it's important to have a clear understanding of what you "should" do and what you "must" do. The "shoulds" are things that would be nice to have or do, but are not essential for the success of your business. The "musts" are the non-negotiable items that are crucial for the survival and success of your business.

For example, you might "should" invest in a fancy office space, but you "must" have a reliable accounting system to keep track of your finances. You "should" attend networking events, but you "must" focus on building relationships with your customers.

It's important to prioritize your "musts" and allocate your resources accordingly, as they are the foundation of your business. By understanding the difference between "shoulds" and "musts", you can make better use of your time, money and energy to grow your business and achieve your goals.

CHAPTER TWENTY-THREE

Blend All Energy at One Point

"Learning is a treasure that will follow its owner everywhere."
— Chinese Proverb

Once upon a time, there was a young man named Tony who was fed up with working for someone else. He had always dreamed of being his own boss, making his own decisions, and living life on his own terms.

One day, Tony decided that it was time to take control of his life. He quit his job and set out to start his own business. At first, he struggled to find his footing. He had no experience running a business, and he found that he was constantly being pulled in different directions.

But Tony refused to give up. He knew that if he wanted to be his own boss, he needed to blend all of his energy at one point. He focused all of his attention and energy on his business, working tirelessly to make it a success. He poured all of his knowledge and skills into the venture, constantly experimenting and adapting to find what worked best.

Over time, Tony's business began to grow. He attracted more customers, and he was able to hire a team of employees to help him manage the day-to-day operations. Tony was now in complete control of his own life, and he was finally living the dream of being his own boss.

As Tony looked back on his journey, he realized that the key to his success had been his unwavering focus and determination. He had blended all of his energy at one point, and that had allowed him to overcome the many obstacles that had stood in his way.

Now, Tony was proud of the life he had built for himself. He was proud to be his own boss, and he was grateful for the lessons he had learned along the way. And he was always happy to share his story with others, hoping to inspire them to follow in his footsteps and pursue their own dreams of entrepreneurship.

Yes, that's correct. Being your own boss requires a lot of focus, energy, and dedication. To be successful, you need to be able to blend all of your energies into a single goal and work towards it relentlessly. This means being able to balance different aspects of your business, such as marketing, sales, operations, and finances, while also taking care of your personal life and well-being.

As an entrepreneur, you are the driving force behind your business, and it's essential to maintain a clear vision of what you want to achieve and stay focused on it. It's also important to stay motivated, even when faced with challenges and obstacles. By bringing all of your energies together and staying focused on your goal, you can overcome any obstacle and achieve success as your own boss.

It's also important to note that being your own boss requires a great deal of self-discipline and time management. You need to be able to set boundaries and prioritize your tasks to ensure that you are using your time effectively. This includes setting aside time for self-care, rest, and recreation, as well as dedicating the time necessary to grow and develop your business.

One need to take action immediately

Yes, taking action immediately is a critical aspect of being your own boss. Entrepreneurship is all about taking action and turning your ideas into reality. Instead of just talking about your ideas or making plans, you need to take action and put them into practice. This can involve conducting market research, creating a business plan, reaching out to potential customers, building a website, and more.

Taking action quickly also means being able to adapt and pivot when necessary. As a business owner, you need to be able to identify and seize opportunities when they arise, and be ready to make changes when circumstances dictate. By taking action immediately, you can stay ahead of the competition and ensure that your business remains relevant and competitive in today's fast-paced business environment.

However, it's also important to strike a balance between taking action and careful planning. While taking immediate action is essential, it's also important to consider the long-term implications of your decisions and ensure that your actions align with your overall business strategy. By combining careful planning with immediate action, you can ensure that your business stays on track and continues to grow and thrive.

One need to take it one oil barrel at a time

Once upon a time, there was a young man named Ali who had always dreamed of being his own boss. He had grown tired of the daily grind of working for someone else, and he longed for the freedom to make his own decisions and chart his own course in life.

One day, Ali decided that it was time to take action. He quit his job and set out to start his own business. But as he began his journey, he soon realized that the road ahead was long and treacherous. He found himself facing a great desert, with no clear path in sight.

Despite the challenges, Ali refused to give up. He knew that if he wanted to be his own boss, he needed to take it one oil barrel at a time. He decided to focus on one task at a time, taking small steps each day to move closer to his goal.

As he traveled across the desert, Ali encountered many obstacles and faced numerous setbacks. But he refused to be discouraged. He reminded himself that success was a journey, not a destination, and that he needed to take one step at a time.

Slowly but surely, Ali began to make progress. He developed a new product that was in high demand, and he soon had a thriving business. He was now in control of his own life, and he was finally living the dream of being his own boss.

As Ali looked back on his journey, he realized that the key to his success had been his perseverance and determination. He had taken it one oil barrel at a time, and that had allowed him to cross the great desert and reach his goal.

Now, Ali was proud of the life he had built for himself. He was proud to be his own boss, and he was grateful for the lessons he had learned along the way. And he was always happy to share his story with others, hoping to inspire them to pursue their own dreams of entrepreneurship and to never give up, no matter how difficult the journey may be.

The phrase "to take it one oil barrel at a time" is often used as a metaphor for approaching a complex task or situation in a gradual and incremental manner, rather than trying to tackle everything at once. This can be a useful approach when starting or running a business, especially if you're feeling overwhelmed or unsure of where to start.

When becoming your own boss, it's important to start by setting achievable goals and taking small, incremental steps towards reaching those goals. This can help you build momentum and make steady progress towards your ultimate vision.

It's also important to be patient and persistent in the face of challenges and obstacles. Becoming your own boss is not always easy, but by taking it one step at a time, you can increase your chances of success and avoid becoming overwhelmed by the task at hand.

One need to cross a great desert

The phrase "to cross a great desert" can be seen as a metaphor for the challenges and difficulties that come with starting and running your own business. Just like crossing a desert can be a long and arduous journey, starting and running a successful business often requires a lot of hard work, dedication, and perseverance.

To be your own boss, you will need to be prepared to face many challenges and overcome obstacles along the way. This may include managing finances, finding and retaining customers, dealing with competition, and maintaining a work-life balance.

However, just like reaching the other side of a desert can be rewarding and fulfilling, the rewards of being your own boss can be significant. This includes having more control over your work, being able to create something meaningful and valuable, and potentially earning a higher income.

So, while starting and running your own business can be a difficult journey, it can also be an extremely rewarding and fulfilling experience if you are willing to put in the effort and face the challenges head-on.

One need to take one step at a time

Yes, taking one step at a time is an important approach when it comes to becoming your own boss. Starting a business can be a complex and overwhelming process, but breaking it down into smaller, manageable tasks can make the journey more manageable.

Here are some steps you can take to become your own boss:

Identify your skills and interests: What are you passionate about? What skills and experiences do you have that you could use to start a business?

Conduct market research: Research your potential customers and competitors to determine the feasibility of your business idea.

Create a business plan: This should include a clear mission statement, financial projections, and a plan for marketing and sales.

Obtain financing: Determine how you will fund your business and make a plan for obtaining the necessary financing.

Launch your business: Start small and scale up as your business grows.

Monitor and adjust your plan: Be prepared to pivot and make changes to your business plan as you learn more about your customers and the market.

By taking these steps one at a time, you can move towards your goal of becoming your own boss in a systematic and manageable way.

CHAPTER TWENTY-FOUR

KPIs and KRAs

"The only person who is educated is the one who has learned how to learn and change." — Carl Rogers

Once upon a time, there was a young man named Richards who worked as an entry-level manager at a software company. Despite having a good salary and job security, Richards was always unsatisfied with his job. He felt like he was just a small cog in a big machine and that he was not making the most of his potential.

One day, Richards came across an article about being your own boss and starting your own business. The idea of being in control of his own destiny and making an impact on the world intrigued him. However, he was intimidated by the thought of starting a business from scratch and the many risks that come with it.

But Richards was a determined individual, and he decided to give it a shot. He quit his job and started his own software development company. At first, things were tough. Richards was working longer hours than ever before, and there was no one to guide him. He struggled to keep up with the demands of running a business, but he never lost sight of his goal.

As time passed, Richards realized that the key to success was to focus on the KPIs (Key Performance Indicators) and KRAs (Key Result Areas) of his business. He started tracking his progress, analyzing the data, and making improvements where necessary. He also sought the advice of successful entrepreneurs and business coaches.

Richards's hard work paid off. His company was growing, and he was able to attract more clients and expand his team. He was now in control of his own destiny, and he was making a real impact on the world. He was finally living the life he had always dreamed of.

The moral of the story is that to be your own boss, one needs to focus on KPIs and KRAs. It is essential to track your progress, analyze the data, and make improvements where necessary. With hard work, determination, and a focus on your goals, you too can achieve success and be in control of your own destiny.

Yes, focusing on Key Performance Indicators (KPIs) is an important aspect of being your own boss. KPIs are metrics that help you track the performance of your business and assess whether you are meeting your goals and objectives. They provide a way to measure the success of your business, identify areas for improvement, and make data-driven decisions to drive growth.

Some common KPIs for small businesses include revenue, profit margins, customer acquisition cost, customer lifetime value, and website traffic. By focusing on these metrics, you can get a clear picture of how your business is performing, what is driving growth, and where you need to focus your efforts to improve.

It's important to note that KPIs are specific to each business and industry, so it's important to identify the KPIs that are most relevant to your business and monitor them closely. This requires setting up systems to track and analyze data, and regularly reviewing the results to make informed decisions and take action. By focusing on KPIs, you can ensure that your business is on track and making progress towards its goals.

One need to focus on KRAs

Yes, focusing on Key Result Areas (KRAs) is an important aspect of being your own boss. KRAs are specific areas of your business that you need to focus on to achieve your goals and objectives. They help you identify what is most important to your business and ensure that you are focusing your efforts on the right tasks.

By defining and focusing on KRAs, you can prioritize your tasks and ensure that you are making progress towards your goals. It also helps you stay focused and avoid getting bogged down by distractions and unimportant tasks. Additionally, by tracking your progress in each KRA, you can assess your performance and make data-driven decisions to drive growth and improve your business.

Some common KRAs for small businesses include sales, marketing, operations, customer service, and finances. By focusing on these areas and setting specific, measurable goals for each, you can ensure that your business is on track and making progress towards its objectives.

It's important to note that KRAs are specific to each business and industry, so it's important to identify the KRAs that are most relevant to your business and monitor them closely. This requires setting up systems to track and analyze data, and regularly reviewing the results to make informed decisions and take action. By focusing on KRAs, you can ensure that your business is aligned with your goals and objectives and making progress towards success.

One need to grade himself

There once lived a man named David who longed to be his own boss. He had a creative mind and was always full of ideas, but he struggled to bring them to fruition. Despite his best efforts, his businesses never seemed to take off and he found himself stuck in a dead-end job.

One day, David came across a book about self-assessment and the importance of grading oneself in order to reach one's goals. Intrigued, David started to put the principles into practice and began evaluating his strengths and weaknesses. He identified the areas where he excelled and the areas where he needed improvement, and he made a plan to work on those weaknesses.

David also started setting goals for himself, both short-term and long-term, and he evaluated his progress regularly. He was amazed at how much his self-assessment and grading helped him improve and grow as a person. He found that by continually evaluating himself, he was able to identify and correct his mistakes, which helped him to reach his goals more efficiently.

With his newfound sense of purpose, David quit his dead-end job and started his own business. He focused on his strengths, worked on his weaknesses, and graded himself regularly to ensure that he was always on the right track. And to his surprise, his business took off and became a huge success.

David's success story served as an inspiration to others and showed that to be your own boss, one needs to be constantly self-aware and grade oneself regularly. By doing so, one can identify their strengths and weaknesses, set achievable goals, and ultimately reach their full potential.

Yes, self-assessment and self-grading is an important aspect of being your own boss. As an entrepreneur, you are ultimately responsible for the success of your business, so it's important to assess your own performance regularly and identify areas for improvement.

Self-assessment involves regularly evaluating your performance in various areas of your business, including sales, marketing, operations, customer service, and finances. You can use tools like SWOT analysis, performance evaluations, and customer feedback to get a clear picture of your strengths and weaknesses and determine what you need to do to improve.

By grading yourself, you can hold yourself accountable for your actions and decisions, and ensure that you are making progress towards your goals. It also helps you identify areas where you need to focus your efforts to improve your skills and knowledge, and develop a plan to address any gaps. Additionally, self-grading can provide valuable insight into your own performance, help you build confidence, and increase your motivation to succeed.

It's important to approach self-assessment objectively, be honest about your strengths and weaknesses, and use the results to inform your decision-making and take action to improve. By regularly grading yourself, you can stay on track and ensure that your business is making progress towards success.

One need to focus on clarity

Yes, having clarity is an important aspect of being your own boss. Clarity refers to having a clear understanding of your goals, objectives, and priorities, and a clear vision of what you want to achieve with your business.

Having clarity helps you make informed decisions and take action in the right direction. It also helps you stay focused and avoid getting bogged down by distractions and unimportant tasks. Additionally, by having clarity, you can communicate your vision and goals effectively to your team and stakeholders, and build a shared understanding of what you're trying to achieve.

To achieve clarity, it's important to define your goals and objectives, and regularly review and revise them as needed. It's also important to regularly assess your progress and make adjustments to your plan as needed. By focusing on clarity, you can ensure that you are making progress towards your goals and achieving the outcomes you want for your business.

Having clarity also involves having a clear understanding of your target market, competition, and unique value proposition. By knowing your target audience and their needs, you can better focus your marketing efforts and create products and services that meet their needs. By understanding your competition, you can stay ahead of the curve and develop strategies to differentiate your business. And by clearly articulating your unique value proposition, you can better communicate the benefits of your business to potential customers.

In summary, clarity is a critical aspect of being your own boss, and helps you make informed decisions, stay focused, and achieve your goals.

One need to invite honest feedback and appraisal

Once upon a time, there was a young woman named Susan who had a passion for entrepreneurship. She had always dreamed of being her own boss, but whenever she tried to start her own business, she struggled to find success. Despite her best efforts, she was never able to take her business to the next level.

One day, Susan met a successful business owner who offered her some advice. The business owner told Susan that in order to be her own boss and reach her full potential, she needed to be open to honest feedback and appraisal. Susan was skeptical at first, but she trusted the business owner and decided to give it a try.

Susan started asking for honest feedback from her colleagues, friends, and family. She was surprised to find that many people were more than willing to offer their opinions and suggestions. Susan took this feedback seriously and used it to improve her business skills. She also began to give herself regular appraisals, which helped her to identify her strengths and weaknesses.

With her newfound understanding of her strengths and weaknesses, Susan was able to focus on what was important and make the necessary changes to her business. Her business started to grow, and before long, she was well on her way to achieving her goal of being her own boss.

Susan's story shows that to be a successful entrepreneur, one must be open to honest feedback and appraisal. By doing so, one can identify their strengths and weaknesses, set achievable goals, and ultimately reach their full potential.

Yes, inviting honest feedback and appraisal is an important aspect of being your own boss. Feedback from others, including customers, employees, partners, and mentors, can provide valuable insights into your business and help you identify areas for improvement.

By inviting honest feedback, you can gain a better understanding of your strengths and weaknesses, and learn how to better serve your customers and improve your business. Feedback can also help you identify gaps in your knowledge or skills, and provide guidance on how to address them.

Additionally, regular appraisal of your performance can help you assess your progress and identify areas where you need to focus your efforts to improve. This can help you stay on track and ensure that you are making progress towards your goals.

It's important to approach feedback and appraisal with an open mind and be receptive to constructive criticism. This requires being honest with yourself and willing to accept and act on the feedback you receive. It's also important to create a culture of openness and trust, where feedback is welcomed and valued, and employees feel comfortable sharing their thoughts and ideas.

In summary, inviting honest feedback and appraisal is a critical aspect of being your own boss, and helps you gain valuable insights, assess your progress, and make informed decisions to drive growth and improve your business.

One need to be realistic about what you can do, with what you have, where you are

Once upon a time, there was a young man named Tom who always dreamt of becoming his own boss. He was tired of working for others and wanted to be in charge of his own destiny. He had always heard that the road to success was to follow your dreams, and that's exactly what he intended to do.

However, Tom soon realized that becoming your own boss was not as easy as it seemed. He had to be realistic about what he could do with what he had, and where he was in life. He had to take a step back and assess his skills, resources, and location.

At first, Tom was discouraged. He had always thought that success was just a matter of working hard and following your dreams. But now he realized that he needed a solid plan and a realistic understanding of his limitations. He couldn't just quit his job and expect success to fall into his lap.

So, Tom got to work. He started by identifying his strengths and weaknesses. He realized that he was good at sales and had a strong network of contacts, but he lacked technical skills and knowledge of the business world. With this newfound understanding, Tom could now focus on developing his skills and building a network of support.

Next, Tom took a look at his resources. He had some savings, but not enough to start a business from scratch. He also realized that he was living in a small town with limited opportunities for growth.

Tom knew that he would need to be creative and resourceful if he was going to make it as his own boss.

Despite the challenges, Tom was determined to succeed. He started by offering his sales services to local businesses on a freelance basis. He worked hard to build his reputation and expand his network. And before he knew it, he had enough clients and income to quit his job and start his own business.

It wasn't easy, but with determination, hard work, and a realistic understanding of his skills, resources, and location, Tom was able to achieve his dream of becoming his own boss. He learned that success is not just about following your dreams, but about being realistic about what you can do with what you have, where you are.

And that's the story of Tom, a young man who followed his dreams and became his own boss. He proved that anything is possible with hard work, determination, and a realistic understanding of your limitations.

Yes, being realistic about what you can do, with what you have, where you are being an important aspect of being your own boss. As an entrepreneur, it's important to have a clear understanding of your resources, including time, money, and expertise, and to use them wisely to achieve your goals.

Being realistic means setting achievable goals and having a realistic plan for how to achieve them. It means being mindful of the limitations of your resources, and making decisions that are aligned with your strengths and capabilities. It also means being honest with yourself about what you can and cannot do, and being willing to ask for help when needed.

Being realistic also involves being mindful of your current circumstances and the external factors that may impact your business. This includes understanding the competitive landscape, the regulatory environment, and the economic conditions. By being aware of these factors, you can make informed decisions and develop strategies that are well-suited to your current situation.

In summary, being realistic about what you can do, with what you have, where you are being a critical aspect of being your own boss. It helps you set achievable goals, make informed decisions, and achieve success by using your resources wisely

CHAPTER TWENTY-FIVE

Accept Digital Transformation

"The more I read, the more I acquire, the more certain I am that I know nothing." — Voltaire

Yes, being ready to accept digital transformation is an important aspect of being your own boss. Digital transformation refers to the integration of digital technology into all areas of a business, leading to fundamental changes to how the business operates and delivers value to customers.

In today's rapidly evolving digital landscape, businesses that are not willing to embrace digital transformation risk being left behind by competitors who are taking advantage of the many benefits of technology. Digital technologies can provide a range of benefits, including increased efficiency, improved customer experiences, and greater access to new markets and revenue streams.

As a business owner, it's important to stay up-to-date with the latest digital technologies and trends, and be willing to embrace new technologies that can help your business succeed. This may require investing in new systems and processes, training employees, and taking the time to understand how new technologies can be used to achieve your goals.

Additionally, being ready to accept digital transformation requires a willingness to experiment and embrace change. This may mean trying new approaches, taking risks, and being open to new ideas. By being open to change and willing to embrace new technologies, you can stay ahead of the curve and ensure the long-term success of your business.

In summary, being ready to accept digital transformation is a critical aspect of being your own boss. It helps you stay competitive, improve your operations, and achieve success in today's rapidly evolving digital landscape.

One need to know technology is wonderful servant

Yes, technology can be a wonderful servant, but a terrible master. When used effectively, technology can improve efficiency, productivity, and collaboration, and help you achieve your goals faster and more easily. However, when technology takes over our lives, it can become a source of stress, distraction, and addiction. To be your own boss, it's important to use technology in a way that supports your goals, rather than hinders them. This means finding a balance between utilizing the benefits of technology and maintaining control over your time and attention. By treating technology as a servant rather than a master, you can create a more fulfilling and sustainable work environment, and achieve greater success and satisfaction as your own boss.

One need to understand latest technologies but not to be addicted to them

Yes, that's an important point. In today's rapidly changing technological landscape, it's crucial to stay informed about the latest tools, techniques, and innovations that can help you grow your business and achieve your goals. However, it's equally important not to become overly reliant on technology and to maintain a healthy balance in your life. Technology can be a great tool for improving efficiency and productivity, but it can also consume a lot of time and energy, and even lead to burnout. To be your own boss, you need to be able to use technology in a strategic and mindful way, and to prioritize your well-being, relationships, and personal growth.

One need take control on your emotions using Technology

While technology can certainly help you manage and regulate your emotions, it is important to note that being your own boss is about much more than just controlling your emotions. Becoming a successful entrepreneur requires a wide range of skills, including:

Strategic thinking and problem solving

Financial management and budgeting

Sales and marketing

Leadership and management

Networking and relationship building

Technology can certainly play a role in helping you develop these skills and achieve your goals as an entrepreneur, but it is not a replacement for hard work, dedication, and a strong work ethic. There are many tools and resources available, such as productivity apps, project management software, and online courses, that can help you stay organized and focused on your goals. However, the key to success as an entrepreneur is taking personal responsibility for your own growth and development, and using technology as a tool to support your progress.

One need to spend more time on software or app which will make you more efficient

Spending time on software or apps that increase efficiency can certainly be a useful tool for entrepreneurs. However, it's important to find the right balance between using technology to streamline processes and not getting bogged down by it. Here are a few tips for using technology effectively as an entrepreneur:

Choose the right tools: There are many productivity and project management tools available, so it's important to choose the ones that are right for your business and your personal working style.

Prioritize: Focus on the tasks that are most important and automate or delegate the rest.

Be mindful of time management: While technology can help you save time in some areas, it's important to avoid spending too much time on non-essential tasks or getting lost in a never-ending cycle of email and social media.

Stay organized: Use technology to stay organized and keep track of your to-do list, deadlines, and projects.

In summary, while technology can be a valuable tool for entrepreneurs, it's important to use it in a way that supports your goals and priorities, and to not get overwhelmed by it. Finding the right balance between technology and other essential elements of running a business, such as networking and relationship building, is key to success as an entrepreneur.

One need to have digital detox for 1 day each week

Having a digital detox, or taking a break from technology, can be an important aspect of maintaining a healthy work-life balance when you're your own boss. Spending too much time on devices can lead to feelings of overwhelm, anxiety, and burnout, and can negatively impact your mental and physical health. By taking a break from technology for one day each week, you can reduce stress, increase productivity, and create more time and space for self-care, creativity, and connection with the people and activities you love. However, it's important to find a balance that works for you, and to make sure that your digital detox doesn't interfere with your work responsibilities or important relationships. A digital detox can be a useful tool for maintaining balance and well-being, but it's just one piece of a larger puzzle, and it's up to each individual to determine what works best for them.

CHAPTER TWENTY-SIX

Personal and Professional Development Goals

"Study hard what interests you the most in the most undisciplined, irreverent and original manner possible." — Richard Feynman

Yes, understanding your personal and professional development goals is an important aspect of being your own boss. Personal development goals refer to the areas of your life that you want to improve, such as your health, relationships, or skills. Professional development goals refer to the skills, knowledge, or experience you want to gain to help you succeed in your business.

Having a clear understanding of your personal and professional development goals can help you stay focused and motivated, and ensure that you are making progress towards the life and career you want. It's important to regularly review and update your goals, and make sure that they are aligned with your values, passions, and long-term vision.

Setting personal and professional development goals also helps you identify areas where you need to improve and provides a roadmap for how to get there. For example, if your goal is to become a better leader, you may need to develop new skills, seek out mentorship or coaching, or engage in continuous learning.

Additionally, personal and professional development goals can help you stay accountable, and provide a sense of direction and purpose. By focusing on your goals and regularly reviewing your progress, you can make informed decisions about how to allocate your time, energy, and resources, and ensure that you are making the most of your opportunities.

In summary, understanding your personal and professional development goals is a critical aspect of being your own boss. It helps you stay focused, motivated, and on track, and ensures that you are making progress towards the life and career you want.

One need to understand family or relationships goal

Yes, understanding your family or relationships goals is an important aspect of being your own boss. Being an entrepreneur can be a rewarding experience, but it can also be demanding and time-consuming, and it's important to ensure that your business pursuits don't come at the expense of your personal relationships.

Having a clear understanding of your family or relationships goals can help you prioritize and balance your time and energy, and ensure that you are making time for the people who matter most to you. This may involve setting goals for spending quality time with family and friends, maintaining strong relationships, or finding ways to support and care for loved ones.

It's important to have open and honest communication with your family and loved ones about your business and personal goals, and to involve them in the decision-making process where possible. This can help you to build a strong support network and ensure that everyone is on the same page.

Additionally, having a clear understanding of your family or relationships goals can help you make informed decisions about your work-life balance, and ensure that you are taking care of your personal needs and well-being. This may involve setting boundaries, delegating responsibilities, and making time for self-care and relaxation.

In summary, understanding your family or relationships goals is a critical aspect of being your own boss. It helps you balance your time and energy, build a strong support network, and ensure that your business pursuits don't come at the expense of your personal relationships.

One need to business or career goals

Yes, having clear business or career goals is an important aspect of being your own boss. Having a clear understanding of your goals can help you stay focused and motivated, and ensure that you are making progress towards the career and business you want.

Business or career goals can be specific and measurable targets, such as increasing your revenue, launching a new product, or expanding into new markets. They can also be broader aspirations, such as creating a business that aligns with your values and passions, or building a company that makes a positive impact on the world.

Having clear business or career goals can help you make informed decisions about how to allocate your time, energy, and resources, and ensure that you are making the most of your opportunities. It's also important to regularly review and update your goals, and make sure that they are aligned with your values, vision, and personal and professional development goals.

In addition, having clear business or career goals can help you stay accountable, and provide a sense of direction and purpose. By focusing on your goals and regularly reviewing your progress, you can make informed decisions about how to allocate your time, energy, and resources, and ensure that you are making the most of your opportunities.

In summary, having clear business or career goals is a critical aspect of being your own boss. It helps you stay focused and motivated, make informed decisions, and ensure that you are making progress towards the career and business you want.

One need to health goals

Yes, having clear health goals is an important aspect of being your own boss. Being an entrepreneur can be a demanding and time-consuming experience, and it's important to prioritize your physical and mental health in order to perform at your best.

Having clear health goals can help you stay focused on taking care of yourself, and ensure that you are making time for self-care and physical activity. This may involve setting goals for regular exercise, eating a healthy diet, getting adequate sleep, and reducing stress.

It's important to recognize that taking care of your health is not just a personal responsibility, but a business necessity. Poor health can impact your energy levels, productivity, and overall well-being, and can negatively impact your business success.

Incorporating healthy habits into your daily routine can help you maintain your energy levels, reduce stress, and improve your overall well-being. This can also have a positive impact on your mood, motivation, and ability to focus, and can help you perform at your best.

In summary, having clear health goals is a critical aspect of being your own boss. It helps you prioritize your physical and mental health, maintain your energy levels, reduce stress, and improve your overall well-being, which are all important factors in your success as an entrepreneur.

One need to understand financial goals

Yes, having a clear understanding of your financial goals is an important aspect of being your own boss. Running a business or being self-employed often involves managing your own finances, and it's important to have a clear understanding of your financial situation, including your income, expenses, and assets.

Having clear financial goals can help you make informed decisions about how to manage your money, and ensure that you are making progress towards financial stability and security. Financial goals can include paying off debt, saving for the future, investing in your business, and building wealth.

In addition, having a clear understanding of your financial situation can help you stay on top of your expenses, manage your cash flow, and make informed decisions about how to allocate your resources.

It's important to regularly review and update your financial goals, and make sure that they are aligned with your personal and business objectives. It's also important to have a plan in place for managing your finances, including creating a budget, tracking your expenses, and seeking advice from a financial advisor if necessary.

In summary, having clear financial goals and a plan for managing your finances is a critical aspect of being your own boss. It helps you make informed decisions about how to manage your money, stay on top of your expenses, and ensure that you are making progress towards financial stability and security.

One need to understand social and community goals

Yes, having a clear understanding of your social and community goals is an important aspect of being your own boss. Building a strong network and actively engaging with your community can have many benefits, including increasing your visibility, expanding your reach, and creating new opportunities for growth and collaboration.

Having clear social and community goals can help you stay focused on building meaningful relationships and actively engaging with your community. This can involve setting goals for networking, volunteering, and participating in community events and activities.

In addition, having a strong sense of purpose and connection to your community can help you stay motivated and inspired, and can provide a sense of fulfilment and satisfaction. It can also help you build a reputation as a leader and influencer in your field, which can have a positive impact on your personal and professional development.

It's important to regularly review and update your social and community goals, and make sure that they are aligned with your personal and business objectives. It's also important to be proactive in building relationships and engaging with your community, and to be open to new opportunities for growth and collaboration.

In summary, having clear social and community goals is a critical aspect of being your own boss. It helps you build a strong network, expand your reach, and create new opportunities for growth and collaboration, and can have a positive impact on your personal and professional development.

One need to understand biggest problems or concerns in life

Yes, understanding your biggest problems or concerns in life is an important aspect of being your own boss. Being self-employed or running a business often involves balancing many different responsibilities and priorities, and it's important to have a clear understanding of what is most important to you.

By identifying your biggest problems or concerns, you can prioritize your time and energy, and ensure that you are making progress in the areas that matter most to you. For example, if one of your biggest concerns is achieving financial stability, you may prioritize activities and projects that will help you increase your income or reduce your expenses.

In addition, understanding your biggest problems or concerns can help you make decisions that are aligned with your values and goals. It can also help you avoid distractions and stay focused on what is most important.

It's important to regularly review and update your understanding of your biggest problems or concerns, and make sure that your actions and priorities are aligned with your values and goals.

In summary, understanding your biggest problems or concerns is a critical aspect of being your own boss. It helps you prioritize your time and energy, make decisions that are aligned with your values and goals, and ensure that you are making progress in the areas that matter most to you.

One need to ask himself to prioritise the goals

Yes, prioritizing your goals is an important aspect of being your own boss. When you have multiple responsibilities and projects, it can be challenging to determine which tasks are most important and deserve your attention first.

By prioritizing your goals, you can make sure that you are focused on the tasks that will have the biggest impact on your business or career. This can involve creating a list of your goals and then ranking them based on their level of importance and urgency.

It's important to regularly review and update your list of priorities, and to adjust your priorities as needed based on changes in your business or personal life.

In addition to helping you stay focused, prioritizing your goals can also help you avoid burnout and stress. When you are focused on the most important tasks, you are more likely to feel productive and accomplished, and less likely to feel overwhelmed or frustrated.

In summary, prioritizing your goals is a critical aspect of being your own boss. It helps you stay focused on the most important tasks, avoid burnout and stress, and feel productive and accomplished.

CHAPTER TWENTY-SEVEN

Time Management and Work Life Balance

"Self-education is, I firmly believe, the only kind of education there is." — Isaac Asimov

Yes, time management and work-life balance are crucial aspects of being your own boss. When you are self-employed or running a business, it can be easy to get caught up in work and neglect other important areas of your life, such as your health, relationships, and personal interests.

Effective time management involves creating a system for organizing and scheduling your tasks, so that you can ensure that you are spending your time on the most important and urgent tasks. This can involve setting clear priorities, delegating tasks, and finding ways to be more productive and efficient.

Work-life balance involves finding the right balance between work and other areas of your life, so that you can feel fulfilled and satisfied both professionally and personally. This can involve setting boundaries between work and personal time, finding ways to reduce stress, and making time for activities and relationships that are important to you.

By understanding the importance of time management and work-life balance, you can create a more sustainable and fulfilling business or career, and avoid burnout and stress.

In summary, time management and work-life balance are not optional for those who want to be their own boss. They are critical aspects of creating a successful and sustainable business or career, and can help you avoid burnout and stress, and feel fulfilled and satisfied both professionally and personally.

Yes, focusing on a few key goals is an important aspect of being your own boss. When you have too many goals, it can be difficult to determine which tasks are most important, and you may end up feeling overwhelmed or frustrated.

By focusing on 3 major goals, you can create a clear and manageable plan for achieving your objectives. This allows you to focus your energy and attention on the most important tasks, and avoid wasting time and resources on tasks that are less critical.

When selecting your 3 major goals, it's important to consider a balance of short-term and long-term objectives, as well as goals in different areas of your life, such as your business or career, personal growth, and relationships.

In order to work on your goals single-mindedly, it's important to set clear and measurable targets, and to regularly track your progress. You should also prioritize tasks and activities that will help you achieve your goals, and eliminate or delegate tasks that are less important or not directly related to your goals.

In summary, focusing on 3 major goals is an effective strategy for those who want to be their own boss. By focusing on a few key objectives, you can create a clear and manageable plan for achieving your goals, and avoid feeling overwhelmed or frustrated.

One need has clean workplace for positive vibes

Having a clean and organized workspace can certainly contribute to a positive and productive work environment, but it is not the only factor necessary to be your own boss.

To be successful as an entrepreneur or self-employed individual, you also need to have:

A clear business plan and strategy

Strong financial management skills

The ability to market and promote your business effectively

A deep understanding of your industry and target market

Strong time management and prioritization skills

A willingness to take risks and adapt to change

Having a clean workplace can help you create a positive and productive environment, but it's just one aspect of the many skills and qualities you need to be your own boss and run a successful business.

Brush-Up The Key Skills Regularly

"Study the past if you would define the future." — Confucius

Yes, upgrading key skills on a regular basis is an important aspect of being your own boss. As your business evolves and the market changes, it's essential to continually develop your skills and knowledge to stay competitive and relevant.

Some key skills you might consider upgrading include:

Financial management: Understanding how to manage your finances, create budgets, and make informed financial decisions is crucial to running a successful business.

Marketing and sales: As your business grows, you'll need to develop your marketing and sales skills to reach and retain customers.

Technology: Technology is rapidly changing, and staying up-to-date with the latest tools and software can help you streamline your business processes and remain competitive.

Leadership: As your business grows, you may need to hire employees and manage teams. Developing your leadership skills can help you build a strong and motivated team.

Networking: Building relationships with other business owners, customers, and industry experts can help you grow your business and access new opportunities.

By regularly upgrading your skills, you can ensure that you have the knowledge and abilities you need to succeed as your own boss.

One need to never stop learning

Yes, that's absolutely true. To be successful as your own boss, you must have a lifelong commitment to learning and personal growth. The business world is constantly changing, and staying ahead of the curve requires continuous learning and improvement.

Here are some ways you can continue learning as a business owner:

Read industry publications and attend trade shows and events to stay up-to-date with the latest trends and developments in your industry.

Take courses and workshops to improve your business skills, such as financial management, marketing, and leadership.

Network with other business owners and industry experts to learn from their experiences and insights.

Seek mentorship from successful entrepreneurs to gain guidance and support as you grow your business.

Experiment and test new ideas and strategies to continuously improve and grow your business.

By embracing a lifelong learning mentality, you can ensure that you have the knowledge and skills you need to succeed as your own boss and build a successful business.

One need to have personal plan to upgrade the skills

Yes, having a personal plan to upgrade your skills is an important aspect of being your own boss. By proactively identifying the skills you need to improve and creating a plan for upgrading them, you can ensure that you have the knowledge and abilities you need to succeed as a business owner.

Here are some steps you can take to create a personal plan for upgrading your skills:

Identify your strengths and weaknesses: Take an honest assessment of your current skills and identify areas where you need to improve.

Set specific goals: Determine what skills you want to upgrade and set specific, measurable goals for improving those skills.

Create a plan: Make a plan for how you will upgrade your skills, including what courses or workshops you will take, what books or publications you will read, and who you will network with.

Schedule time for learning and improvement: Make learning and improvement a priority by scheduling dedicated time for it in your calendar.

Track your progress: Regularly evaluate your progress towards your goals and make adjustments to your plan as needed.

By following these steps, you can create a personalized plan for upgrading your skills and continuously improving as a business owner. This will help you build the knowledge and abilities you need to succeed and grow your business over time.

CHAPTER TWENTY-NINE

Good Active Listening

"Education is the passport to the future, for tomorrow belongs to those who prepare for it today." — Malcolm X

Yes, having good listening skills is important for anyone who wants to be their own boss. As a business owner, you need to be able to listen to and understand your customers, employees, and partners to ensure that you're providing the products and services they need and that your business is running smoothly.

Here are some ways that having good listening skills can benefit you as a business owner:

Improving customer satisfaction: By actively listening to your customers and understanding their needs and concerns, you can improve customer satisfaction and build strong, lasting relationships with your customers.

Solving problems: Good listening skills can help you identify and resolve problems in your business more effectively, by allowing you to understand the root causes of problems and find the best solutions.

Building trust: When you listen actively and show that you care about what others are saying, you build trust and credibility with your employees, partners, and customers.

One need to know technology can take control of your communications

Yes, that's a very important point. Technology has revolutionized the way we communicate, but it can also take over our lives if we're not careful. With the constant barrage of emails, messages, and notifications, it can be easy to feel like we're always "on" and never fully present. This can lead to burnout, decreased productivity, and strained relationships. To be your own boss, it's important to understand that technology can take control of your communications and to use it in a way that supports, rather than hinders, your goals and well-being. This can involve setting boundaries, such as only checking email at certain times of the day, turning off notifications during focused work periods, or taking regular breaks from screens. By taking control of your communications, you can maintain a healthy balance, communicate effectively with clients and colleagues, and achieve greater success as your own boss.

CHAPTER THIRTY

Thought Leadership

"Education is the most powerful weapon which you can use to change the world." — Nelson Mandela

Yes, having thought leadership skills can be highly beneficial for anyone who wants to be their own boss. Thought leadership involves having a deep understanding of your industry, and being able to communicate that knowledge in a compelling and influential way.

Here are some benefits of having strong thought leadership skills:

Establishing expertise: By demonstrating your knowledge and expertise in your industry, you can establish yourself as a trusted and respected leader and build a strong reputation in your market.

Attracting customers: Thought leaders are often seen as thought leaders in their industries, which can attract new customers and business opportunities.

Differentiating from competitors: By being a recognized thought leader, you can differentiate yourself from your competition and set yourself apart as a unique and valuable player in your market.

Driving innovation: Thought leaders are often at the forefront of new and innovative ideas and trends, and by embracing that role, you can drive innovation in your industry and keep your business ahead of the curve.

Building a personal brand: Thought leadership can also help you build a personal brand and increase your visibility and credibility as a business owner.

By developing your thought leadership skills, you can become a recognized and respected leader in your industry, and set your business on a path to success.

CHAPTER THIRTY-ONE

Identify Your Key Constraints

"As we look ahead into the next century, leaders will be those who empower others." — Bill Gates

Yes, identifying your key constraints is an important step in becoming your own boss. Some common constraints that entrepreneurs face include:

Lack of capital: Starting a business often requires a significant amount of financial investment, and securing funding can be a major constraint for many entrepreneurs.

Limited experience or skills: Entrepreneurs may not have the necessary experience or expertise to successfully launch and run a business, which can also be a constraint.

Competition: The market may already be crowded with established players, making it difficult for a new business to gain a foothold.

Lack of resources: Entrepreneurs may not have access to the resources they need, such as personnel, equipment, or technology, to effectively launch and grow their business.

Regulatory environment: Governments and other regulatory bodies can create constraints for entrepreneurs by setting rules and regulations that must be followed in order to operate a business.

By identifying these and other key constraints, entrepreneurs can develop strategies to overcome them and increase their chances of success. This might involve seeking out additional funding sources, partnering with more experienced individuals, or finding creative solutions to resource constraints.

One need to identify limiting factor

Yes, identifying limiting factors is also an important step in becoming your own boss. Limiting factors refer to anything that prevents you from achieving your goals or reaching your full potential as a business owner. These factors can range from internal limitations, such as a lack of experience or skills, to external constraints, such as economic conditions or market competition.

Some common limiting factors that entrepreneurs may face include:

Time: Entrepreneurs often wear many hats and have limited time to focus on growing their business.

Cash flow: Insufficient cash flow can limit a business's ability to make necessary investments, pay bills, and manage growth.

Talent: Finding and retaining the right employees can be a challenge for small businesses, especially in competitive industries.

Market conditions: External factors, such as economic conditions, changes in consumer behavior, or new competition, can limit a business's growth and success.

Technology: A lack of access to the latest technology or tools can limit a business's ability to compete and innovate.

By identifying and addressing these limiting factors, entrepreneurs can build a stronger, more resilient business and increase their chances of success. This might involve finding ways to improve cash flow, developing new strategies for attracting and retaining top talent, or investing in new technology.

One need answer what is it in me that is holding me back

Yes, answering the question "what is it in me that is holding me back?" is an important step in becoming your own boss. Self-awareness and introspection can help you identify your personal limitations and develop strategies to overcome them.

Some common internal factors that can hold entrepreneurs back include:

Lack of confidence: Entrepreneurs may struggle with self-doubt and a lack of confidence in their abilities, which can limit their success.

Fear of failure: The fear of failure can prevent entrepreneurs from taking risks and pursuing new opportunities.

Resistance to change: Entrepreneurs may struggle with change and be resistant to trying new things or adapting to new situations.

Perfectionism: A tendency to focus on perfection rather than progress can limit a business's growth and success.

Procrastination: Procrastination can prevent entrepreneurs from taking action and following through on their plans and goals.

By recognizing and overcoming these internal limitations, entrepreneurs can build a stronger, more resilient business and increase their chances of success. This might involve seeking out opportunities for personal development, working with a coach or mentor, or finding new ways to build confidence and tackle fear.

One need to strive for accuracy

Yes, striving for accuracy is an important aspect of being your own boss. Accurate information, record-keeping, and reporting are essential for making informed business decisions, building trust with customers and partners, and ensuring the success of your business.

Here are some ways that striving for accuracy can benefit entrepreneurs:

Improved decision making: Accurate information and data can help entrepreneurs make informed decisions about their business, such as identifying trends, evaluating performance, and tracking progress.

Increased efficiency: Accurate record-keeping and reporting can help entrepreneurs streamline their processes, save time, and reduce errors.

Better relationships: Staying accurate with customers, suppliers, and partners can build trust and help maintain strong relationships.

Compliance with regulations: Accurate record-keeping and reporting are often required by law, and can help entrepreneurs avoid penalties and other legal consequences.

Increased credibility: A reputation for accuracy and attention to detail can increase the credibility of a business and help it stand out in a crowded market.

Striving for accuracy is a key aspect of responsible and effective business management, and can play a critical role in the success of an entrepreneurial venture.

One need to apply Pareto principle on constraints

Yes, applying the Pareto principle, also known as the 80/20 rule, to constraints can be an effective way for entrepreneurs to prioritize their efforts and make the most impact.

The Pareto principle states that roughly 80% of the effects come from 20% of the causes. In the context of business, this principle can be applied to constraints by focusing on the 20% of constraints that are causing the majority of problems or hindering growth.

Here are some steps for applying the Pareto principle to constraints:

Identify your constraints: Start by listing out all the constraints that are holding back your business, whether they are internal or external.

Prioritize your constraints: Rank your constraints in order of importance, based on the impact they are having on your business.

Focus on the key constraints: Focus your attention on the 20% of constraints that are having the greatest impact on your business.

Develop solutions: Work on finding solutions to the most impactful constraints, whether it be through process improvements, new technology, or partnerships.

By focusing on the most impactful constraints, entrepreneurs can maximize their efforts and make the greatest impact on their business. The Pareto principle can be a helpful tool for entrepreneurs looking to streamline their operations, increase efficiency, and overcome the obstacles holding back their business.

CHAPTER THIRTY-TWO

Concentrate On Mental Strength

"That is what learning is. You suddenly understand something you've understood all your life, but in a new way." — Doris Lessing

Yes, mental strength is a critical component of being your own boss. As an entrepreneur or self-employed individual, you will face numerous challenges, obstacles, and difficult decisions. Having mental fortitude will help you stay focused, motivated, and resilient in the face of these obstacles.

To develop your mental strength, you can practice the following:

Mindfulness and self-reflection: Take time to reflect on your thoughts, emotions, and actions, and develop an awareness of how they impact your well-being and work.

Positive self-talk: Speak to yourself in a positive, supportive, and encouraging manner.

Goal setting: Clearly define your goals and develop a plan to achieve them.

Time management: Effectively manage your time to ensure you are able to balance work and personal life.

Resilience: Learn to bounce back from setbacks and failures, and develop a growth mind-set that embraces challenges as opportunities for growth.

In summary, mental strength is essential for success as a self-employed individual. By focusing on building your mental fortitude, you can increase your chances of success and enjoy the many benefits of being your own boss.

One need to put the pressure on yourself

Yes, as a self-employed individual, you need to put pressure on yourself to be successful. When you are your own boss, there is no one else to hold you accountable for your actions and results. This means that you need to take responsibility for your own success and be proactive in achieving your goals.

Putting pressure on yourself can help you stay focused, motivated, and driven to succeed. It can also help you develop a strong work ethic and a sense of self-discipline. However, it's important to avoid putting too much pressure on yourself, as this can lead to burnout, stress, and decreased productivity.

To balance the pressure, you can:

Set realistic and achievable goals: Break down your long-term goals into smaller, manageable tasks and celebrate your progress along the way.

Prioritize self-care: Make time for yourself to rest, recharge, and engage in activities that bring you joy and fulfilment.

Seek support: Connect with others in your industry or community, and seek advice and support from mentors, friends, and family.

Practice flexibility: Be open to change and adapt to new circumstances and challenges.

By putting pressure on yourself in a balanced and healthy way, you can stay motivated and achieve your goals as a self-employed individual.

One need beat their own imaginary deadlines

Yes, setting and meeting your own deadlines can be an important aspect of being your own boss. When you are self-employed, there may not be a boss or external authority setting deadlines for you, so it's important to take the initiative and set your own deadlines to ensure you complete projects and tasks on time.

By setting your own deadlines, you can increase your productivity, stay on track, and meet your goals. Additionally, meeting your own deadlines can give you a sense of accomplishment and boost your confidence in your abilities as a self-employed individual.

However, it's important to set realistic and achievable deadlines, rather than deadlines that are too aggressive and difficult to meet. If you find that you are consistently missing your own deadlines, it may be a sign that you need to reassess your goals and priorities, or seek additional support to help you achieve your objectives.

In summary, setting and meeting your own deadlines can be a critical component of success as a self-employed individual. By taking the initiative to set your own deadlines, you can increase your productivity, stay on track, and achieve your goals.

One need more productive

Yes, being productive is a key aspect of being your own boss. When you are self-employed, you need to make the most of your time and resources to achieve your goals and succeed in your business or profession.

There are several ways to increase your productivity, including:

Time management: Create a schedule and prioritize your tasks to make the most of your time.

Eliminate distractions: Minimize distractions, such as email and social media, and focus on the tasks that are most important to your success.

Set achievable goals: Break down larger goals into smaller, manageable tasks, and focus on one task at a time.

Delegation: Delegate tasks to others, such as employees or contractors, to free up time for other tasks that require your attention.

Automation: Use technology and tools to automate routine tasks and save time.

Continuous improvement: Regularly evaluate your productivity and make changes as needed to increase efficiency.

In summary, being productive is essential for success as a self-employed individual. By making the most of your time and resources, you can increase your chances of success and achieve your goals.

One need to find Supreme joy in motivating yourself

Yes, finding joy in motivating yourself is an important aspect of being your own boss. When you are self-employed, you are the driving force behind your own success, and you need to be able to motivate yourself on a daily basis to achieve your goals.

Finding joy in motivation can help you stay positive, focused, and driven, even when faced with challenges and setbacks. Here are some tips to help you find joy in motivating yourself:

Set meaningful goals: Choose goals that align with your passions and values, and that bring you a sense of purpose and fulfilment.

Focus on progress, not perfection: Celebrate your small wins and progress along the way, rather than only focusing on the end goal.

Surround yourself with positivity: Surround yourself with people and resources that inspire and support you.

Cultivate a growth mind-set: Embrace challenges and setbacks as opportunities for growth and learning.

Practice gratitude: Take time to appreciate what you have and reflect on your accomplishments.

By finding joy in motivating yourself, you can maintain a positive and driven mind-set, and increase your chances of success as a self-employed individual.

One need boost self esteem

Yes, having a healthy level of self-esteem is important for success as a self-employed individual. Self-esteem refers to the way we feel about ourselves, and a high level of self-esteem can help you feel confident, capable, and resilient in the face of challenges.

Here are some ways to boost your self-esteem as a self-employed individual:

Set and achieve small goals: Accomplishing small tasks and goals can help you build confidence and feel a sense of achievement.

Practice self-care: Taking care of your physical and emotional well-being can help you feel better about yourself and increase your self-esteem.

Surround yourself with positive people: Surround yourself with people who support and encourage you, and avoid those who bring you down.

Focus on your strengths: Identify your unique skills and strengths, and focus on using them to contribute to your success.

Learn from mistakes: Instead of dwelling on mistakes, see them as opportunities for learning and growth.

Embrace positive self-talk: Speak kindly and positively to yourself, and challenge negative self-talk.

Boosting your self-esteem can help you feel confident and capable in your work as a self-employed individual, and increase your chances of success.

One need to only think and talk about the things you want rather than the things you don't want

Yes, focusing on what you want, rather than what you don't want, can be an important aspect of being your own boss. This mind-set, often referred to as a "positive focus," can help you stay motivated and optimistic, even in the face of challenges.

By focusing on what you want, you can stay focused on your goals and vision for your business or career, and avoid getting bogged down by negative thoughts and distractions. This can help you maintain a positive and proactive mindset, and increase your chances of success.

One need to know people management

Yes, knowing how to effectively manage people is an important aspect of being your own boss. As a self-employed individual, you may be responsible for managing employees, contractors, or team members, and your ability to effectively lead and manage others can have a significant impact on your success.

Here are some key skills and strategies for effective people management:

Communication: Develop clear and effective communication skills, and listen to your team members' needs and concerns.

Motivation: Find ways to motivate and inspire your team members to work together towards common goals.

Leadership: Lead by example, and provide clear direction and guidance for your team.

Delegation: Learn how to delegate tasks effectively, and give your team members the resources and support they need to succeed.

Performance management: Set clear expectations and performance standards, and provide regular feedback and coaching to your team members.

Conflict resolution: Be prepared to resolve conflicts and disagreements within your team, and maintain a positive and productive work environment.

In summary, knowing how to effectively manage people is an important aspect of being a successful self-employed individual. By developing your leadership and people management skills, you can build a strong and productive team, and increase your chances of success.

One need process management

Yes, effective process management is an important aspect of being your own boss. As a self-employed individual, you will likely be responsible for managing many different aspects of your business, from finances and operations to marketing and sales. Having clear processes in place can help you streamline your work and improve your productivity.

Here are some tips for effective process management as a self-employed individual:

Identify your key processes: Identify the key processes in your business, such as product development, customer service, and accounting.

Document and standardize your processes: Document each process in detail, and establish clear standards and procedures for how work should be done.

Continuously improve your processes: Regularly review and assess your processes, and look for ways to improve them and make them more efficient.

Automate where possible: Consider using technology and automation tools to streamline your processes and reduce manual work.

Foster a culture of continuous improvement: Encourage your team members to continuously evaluate and improve your processes, and be open to feedback and suggestions.

In summary, effective process management is an important aspect of being a successful self-employed individual. By having clear and efficient processes in place, you can improve your productivity, reduce errors and inconsistencies, and increase your chances of success.

One need to know product management

Yes, knowing how to effectively manage your products is an important aspect of being your own boss. As a self-employed individual, you may be responsible for developing and launching new products, managing existing products, and ensuring that your products meet customer needs and deliver value.

Here are some key skills and strategies for effective product management:

Market research: Conduct market research to understand customer needs and trends, and to identify potential opportunities for new products.

Product development: Develop new products that meet customer needs and deliver value, using an iterative process that includes prototyping, testing, and refinement.

Product positioning and differentiation: Position and differentiate your products in the market, and clearly communicate the unique value that they offer to customers.

Pricing strategy: Develop a pricing strategy that balances profitability with customer value and demand.

Product launch and go-to-market strategy: Plan and execute a successful product launch, and develop a go-to-market strategy that effectively reaches and converts customers.

Product life cycle management: Manage the life cycle of your products, from development and launch to maturity and decline, and make informed decisions about when to discontinue products that are no longer profitable.

In summary, knowing how to effectively manage your products is an important aspect of being a successful self-employed individual. By having a strong understanding of product management principles and strategies, you can increase your chances of success and deliver value to your customers.

CHAPTER THIRTY-THREE

Pick up Things by Choice. Not by Chance!!

"Success is no accident. It is hard work, perseverance, learning, studying, sacrifice and most of all, love of what you are doing or learning to do." — Pele

Yes, that's correct. Being your own boss requires taking responsibility for your career and financial success, and making informed choices about the work you do and the businesses you start. It's important to have a clear understanding of your strengths, weaknesses, and passions, and to find a business idea that aligns with your skills and interests. You must also be prepared to put in the time and effort required to build and grow your business, and to manage the risks and challenges that come with entrepreneurship. By taking control of your career and making deliberate choices, you can achieve the independence and satisfaction that comes with being your own boss.

One need to refuse to be a Slave

Yes, in a way, being your own boss involves refusing to be a slave to someone else's vision and goals. When you work for someone else, you are limited by their priorities, rules, and expectations. You may not have control over the direction of your career or the impact of your work. By starting your own business or becoming a freelancer, you have the freedom to set your own goals, choose the projects that excite you, and make decisions that align with your values and aspirations. This gives you greater autonomy and fulfilment in your work. However, it's important to keep in mind that being your own boss also involves taking on greater responsibility, including financial risk and the need to continually adapt to changing circumstances.

One need to take back your time

Yes, taking back control of your time is an important aspect of being your own boss. When you work for someone else, your time is often not your own, and you may feel like you're always rushing from one task to the next, with little time to reflect or recharge. However, when you're your own boss, you have the opportunity to create a work schedule that works for you, and to prioritize the activities that are most important to you. This can include taking breaks, pursuing personal interests, or spending time with loved ones. By taking back your time, you can increase your happiness, reduce stress, and create a more fulfilling work-life balance. It's important to remember, however, that being your own boss also requires discipline, focus, and the ability to manage your time effectively to achieve your goals and grow your business.

One need to be well informed on most of your domain of work

Yes, it's important to have a strong understanding of your industry and the work you do. When you're your own boss, you are responsible for making informed decisions that impact your business and your clients. This requires keeping up with the latest developments, trends, and best practices in your field. It's also important to continuously improve your skills and knowledge so that you can offer high-quality services and stay competitive in your market. By being well-informed and committed to lifelong learning, you can build a successful and rewarding career as your own boss.

One does not need to shift attention back and forth in lollypop of multitasking

Yes, focusing on mental strength is important for entrepreneurs, and shifting attention back and forth between multiple tasks, commonly referred to as multitasking, can be detrimental to one's mental and physical well-being. Research has shown that multitasking can lead to increased stress, decreased productivity, and impaired cognitive function.

Instead of multitasking, entrepreneurs can benefit from developing a growth mind-set and focusing on mental strength by:

Prioritizing self-care: Taking care of physical and mental health through exercise, sleep, and other self-care practices can help entrepreneurs stay focused and motivated.

Cultivating mindfulness: Mindfulness practices such as meditation, deep breathing, or yoga can help entrepreneurs stay present, calm, and centered in the moment.

Developing resilience: Building resilience through practices such as setting realistic goals, learning from failures, and seeking out support can help entrepreneurs stay motivated and focused, even in the face of adversity.

Focusing on one task at a time: Entrepreneurs can improve their focus and productivity by eliminating distractions, and focusing on one task at a time until it is completed.

By focusing on mental strength and developing a growth mind-set, entrepreneurs can increase their chances of success and improve their overall well-being.

CHAPTER THIRTY-FOUR

Slice and Dice the Task

"The purpose of learning is growth, and our minds, unlike our bodies, can continue growing as we continue to live." — Mortimer Adler

Yes, slicing and dicing tasks is a key aspect of time management and productivity for entrepreneurs. Breaking down larger tasks into smaller, manageable chunks can make it easier to stay focused, prioritize, and make progress towards your goals. Here are a few tips for slicing and dicing tasks effectively:

Prioritize: Identify the most important tasks and break them down into smaller steps. Focus on completing these tasks first before moving on to less important tasks.

Set deadlines: Give yourself deadlines for completing each task or step. This can help you stay on track and avoid procrastination.

Use a task list or project management tool: Write down each task or step and keep track of your progress. This can help you stay organized and ensure that you don't forget anything.

Delegate: Consider delegating some tasks to others, either within your organization or to freelancers or contractors. This can help you focus on the most important tasks and make the most of your time.

Slicing and dicing tasks is an effective way to manage your time and increase productivity as an entrepreneur. By breaking down larger tasks into smaller, manageable steps, you can focus on what is most important, stay organized, and make progress towards your goals.

One need work on salami slice method

The salami slice method is a time management technique that involves breaking down larger tasks into smaller, manageable steps. This method can be a useful tool for entrepreneurs who want to increase their productivity and manage their time more effectively.

Here's how the salami slice method works:

Break down the task: Divide the larger task into smaller, manageable steps or subtasks.

Prioritize: Identify the most important steps and prioritize them based on their urgency and importance.

Focus: Tackle one step at a time, focusing on completing that step before moving on to the next.

Celebrate progress: Celebrate your progress along the way, no matter how small the step. This can help keep you motivated and focused.

By using the salami slice method, entrepreneurs can break down large, daunting tasks into smaller, more manageable steps. This can help them focus on what is most important, prioritize their time, and make progress towards their goals. Additionally, the technique can help entrepreneurs avoid feeling overwhelmed by the sheer size of a task and instead focus on taking small, manageable steps towards completion.

One need work on Swiss cheese method

The Swiss cheese method is a time management technique that involves breaking down larger tasks into smaller, manageable steps, similar to the salami slice method. The difference with the Swiss cheese method is that it incorporates regular breaks and rest periods into the process.

Here's how the Swiss cheese method works:

Break down the task: Divide the larger task into smaller, manageable steps or subtasks.

Prioritize: Identify the most important steps and prioritize them based on their urgency and importance.

Work in short bursts: Work on each step for a set amount of time, and then take a short break. This can help you stay focused and avoid burnout.

Celebrate progress: Celebrate your progress along the way, no matter how small the step. This can help keep you motivated and focused.

By using the Swiss cheese method, entrepreneurs can break down large, daunting tasks into smaller, more manageable steps, and also incorporate rest and breaks into their workday to help them stay focused and avoid burnout. This technique can help entrepreneurs avoid feeling overwhelmed by the sheer size of a task, and instead focus on taking small, manageable steps towards completion, while also allowing for regular rest periods to recharge and maintain focus.

One need to use a time planner

Using a time planner can be a valuable tool for entrepreneurs who want to manage their time effectively and increase their productivity. Here are a few tips for using a time planner effectively:

Schedule your day: Use your time planner to schedule your day, including work tasks, appointments, and personal activities.

Prioritize: Make sure to prioritize your tasks based on their importance and urgency.

Be realistic: Be mindful of your schedule and make sure to allocate enough time for each task. Don't overbook yourself, as this can lead to stress and burnout.

Review your progress: Regularly review your progress and adjust your schedule as needed. This can help you stay on track and make changes to your routine as necessary.

Use technology: Consider using a digital time planner or a productivity app that integrates with your calendar to help you stay organized and on track.

By using a time planner, entrepreneurs can stay organized, prioritize their time, and make progress towards their goals. Whether you use a traditional paper planner or a digital app, the key is to find a tool that works for you and to use it regularly to help you manage your time and stay on track.

One need to use compulsion to closure

Compulsion to closure is the drive to complete tasks and reach closure or completion. This drive can be a valuable tool for entrepreneurs who want to increase their productivity and manage their time effectively.

Here are a few ways to harness your compulsion to closure to help you be more productive:

Set achievable goals: Start by setting small, achievable goals for yourself. This can help you get started and build momentum, and also give you a sense of accomplishment and satisfaction.

Break tasks into smaller steps: Break down larger tasks into smaller, manageable steps to help you make progress and avoid feeling overwhelmed.

Focus on one task at a time: Focus on completing one task before moving on to the next, rather than trying to multitask. This can help you stay focused and avoid distractions.

Use a timer: Set a timer for a specific amount of time and work on a task until the timer goes off. This can help you stay focused and avoid procrastination.

Celebrate completion: Celebrate your progress and the completion of each task, no matter how small. This can help keep you motivated and focused.

By harnessing your compulsion to closure, entrepreneurs can increase their productivity, manage their time effectively, and make progress towards their goals. By setting achievable goals, breaking tasks into smaller steps, focusing on one task at a time, using a timer, and celebrating completion, entrepreneurs can make the most of their time and achieve their goals.

One need to make every minute count

Yes, that's correct. Being an entrepreneur or self-employed requires effective time management, setting and achieving goals, and making the most of every opportunity to grow the business.

One need to control the anger

Yes, controlling anger and emotional management is also an important aspect of being a successful entrepreneur. It allows for better decision making, improved relationships with clients and partners, and a more positive work environment.

One need to build up a sense of momentum

Yes, building momentum is important for entrepreneurs. It helps in creating a positive work culture, establishing a routine, and achieving success faster. Having a sense of momentum also provides motivation and inspiration to keep working towards your goals.

One need to take responsibility

Yes, taking responsibility is a crucial aspect of being a successful entrepreneur. This involves being accountable for your actions, decisions, and the success or failure of the business. Taking responsibility helps build credibility, trust, and a positive reputation, which are all important for the growth and success of a business.

One need to see opportunity or problem and take action immediately

Yes, recognizing opportunities or problems and taking prompt action is a key characteristic of successful entrepreneurs. This ability to act quickly and effectively helps entrepreneurs make the most of opportunities, overcome challenges, and stay ahead of the competition. It also demonstrates their leadership skills and their ability to drive the business forward.

one should have sense of urgency

Yes, having a sense of urgency is important for entrepreneurs. It helps in prioritizing tasks, making quick decisions, and staying focused on the most important goals. A sense of urgency also helps entrepreneurs to keep moving forward and avoid procrastination, which can lead to missed opportunities or problems going unresolved.

one should get going keep going attitude

Yes, having a "get going and keep going" attitude is essential for entrepreneurs. It involves being proactive, persistent, and continuously pushing forward towards success, even in the face of setbacks or challenges. This positive and determined mind-set is critical for overcoming obstacles, adapting to change, and achieving long-term success.

One need to be self-disciplined dedicated and devoted to the goals and task

Yes, being self-disciplined, dedicated, and devoted to your goals and tasks is crucial for entrepreneurship success. It requires setting priorities, establishing a routine, and consistently putting in the time and effort necessary to achieve your goals. This level of dedication and commitment demonstrates a strong work ethic and a passion for the business, which are essential qualities for entrepreneurs.

One need to understand don't waste your time

Yes, understanding the importance of time management is crucial for entrepreneurs. Being efficient with time helps in maximizing productivity, staying focused on important tasks, and avoiding distractions. Effective time management also helps entrepreneurs balance the demands of their personal and professional lives, ensuring they are able to give their best to both.

One need to understand personal management to evolving a personality

Yes, understanding and managing personal development is important for entrepreneurs. This involves continuously learning and growing, both professionally and personally. It requires setting goals, seeking new experiences, and being open to feedback and constructive criticism. Personal development also helps entrepreneurs develop better communication skills, leadership abilities, and emotional intelligence, which are all critical for success in business and life.

CHAPTER THIRTY-FIVE

Conclusion

"A 'genius' is often merely a talented person who has done all of his or her homework." — Thomas Edison

In this book, we have explored the concepts of "Your life, your choice" and "be your own boss". We have seen how taking control of your life and making informed decisions can lead to a fulfilling and meaningful future, where you have the freedom to pursue your passions and shape your own success.

We have also discussed the importance of identifying your goals, developing a plan to achieve them, and taking action to turn your dreams into reality. And, we have touched on the challenges and obstacles that you may encounter along the way and provided strategies for overcoming them.

As you come to the end of this book, we hope that you have a newfound sense of purpose and the confidence to take control of your life and be your own boss. Remember that success is not something that is handed to you, but something that you create for yourself through hard work and determination.

So, embrace the power of "Your life, your choice" and start making the choices that will lead you towards the life you want. Whether you're starting a business, changing careers, or simply seeking greater fulfillment, the choices you make today will determine the future you create for yourself.

So, go out there and make your dreams a reality. Your life, your choice, be your own boss.

www.ingramcontent.com/pod-product-compliance
Lightning Source LLC
Chambersburg PA
CBHW062216150726
47991CB00006B/2301